MARCH INTO
MEATH

MARCH INTO
MEATH
In the Footsteps of 1798

EAMON DOYLE

The History Press Ireland

For Conor, Laoise and Eoghan

'Twixt Croghan–Kinsella and Hook Head, twixt Carnsore and Mount Leinster, there is as good a mass of men as ever sustained a state by honest franchises, by peace, virtue, and intelligent industry; and as stout a mass as ever tramped through stubborn battle. There is a county where we might seek more of stormy romance, and there is a county where prospers a shrewder economy, but no county in Ireland is fitter for freedom than Wexford.'

Thomas Davis, *The Nation*

'From the wild burst with which ye triumphed at Oulart Hill, down to the faint gasp wherewith the last of your column died in the cornfields of Meath, there is nothing to shame your valour, your faith, or your patriotism.'

Thomas Davis, *Centenary Memoir*

First published 2011

The History Press Ireland
119 Lower Baggot Street
Dublin 2
Ireland
www.thehistorypress.ie

© Eamon Doyle, 2011

The right of Eamon Doyle to be identified as the Author
of this work has been asserted in accordance with the
Copyrights, Designs and Patents Act 1988.

British Library Cataloguing in Publication Data.
A catalogue record for this book is available from the British Library.

ISBN 978 1 84588 692 9

Typesetting and origination by The History Press
Printed in Great Britain
Manufacturing managed by Jellyfish Print Solutions Ltd

Contents

Foreword

The march of the surviving 1798 insurgents from Wexford through Wicklow, Kildare, County Meath and then back towards Dublin, has been regarded as an act of madness, incurable optimism, desperation or, in Government eyes, as the flight path of outlaws on the run. The major field battles of the south-east were over and lost. Many exhausted rebels of the May and June campaigns in 1798 had simply gone back to their homes, hid until it was safe to resume work or were caught, killed or transported. So to a great many historians, commentators and sympathisers alike, the question raised with the luxury of hindsight was 'why?'.

The response to the query is that these informed and committed United Irish leadership expected French reinforcements to arrive. It was only a matter of holding out. How best to hold out, and where, was the question. Edward Fitzgerald, Garrett Byrne, Anthony Perry, Esmond Kyan, Edward Roche and Fr Mogue Kearns, with their men, decided to head north from Wicklow. They were hopeful of attracting the thousands they knew to be active United men in the counties around Dublin city to their division and, more significantly still, they looked to link with the United men of Down and Antrim. They did not know that the revolt in the north had been overwhelmed, nor indeed that the propagandists had successfully portrayed their struggle in arms as an extermination campaign against Protestants.

Despite the loss that they did not anticipate, this last fighting division of the United Irishmen in the east must be regarded with unqualified admiration for bravery, for commitment, for determination and for a fighting spirit that brought honour upon themselves and their cause.

The leaders and men were all from working-class livestyles to various degrees. They were not professional soldiers, yet, in the year of their enterprise in arms, there emerged from among their leaders and men some who would adorn in distinction any age, any phase, any decade in Ireland's or Europe's history.

In this book Eamon Doyle marches with these brave men. He takes the reader along with him in their footsteps, in their engagements, in their falling and to their graves. It is a work by a researcher who, from his Athlone base, has undertaken meticulous field research over the miles of their long march. His devotion to his task is evident on every page. Every page offers an invitation to the reader to follow those very same footsteps in the years ahead whenever future generations seek inspiration. The sacrifices freely and gladly made by Irishmen for their country's liberty cannot be better exemplified than in those recorded pages. By the author's justifiable determination to honour them their spirits march through Wicklow, Kildare and Royal Meath once more.

Nicholas Furlong, Wexford

Acknowledgements

I wish to express my grateful thanks to a number of individuals and institutions who were of assistance to me in researching this book. Amongst them are the staff of the National Library of Ireland, the National Archives of Ireland and the Department of Irish Folklore, the staff of County Libraries at Newbridge (Kildare), Edenderry (Offaly), Navan (Meath) and Mullingar (Westmeath).

Thanks to Fr Paul Connell for allowing me access to, and use of, the archives of St Finian's College, Mullingar, and to the many individuals who gave me local direction and information. These include Miss Connolly, Ardmullen; Monsignor E. Marran, Kinnegad; Michael Geraghty, Ballinla, Coralstown; William Beatty, Ballindoolin; Noel Whelan, Edenderry; Andy Bennett, Navan; Oliver Ward, Nobber; Fr Kelly, Athboy; John Robinson, Kilrathmurray; Shiela Crehan, Slane and Anna Kinsella, Courtown.

My thanks to Brian Doyle for all his help with IT, photographs, maps and other mysteries of modern technology.

My thanks to Mr Peter Murphy of Blanchardstown who kindly supplied, and allowed me to use, material collected by his father, Garda Richard Murphy.

Very special thanks is due to Dr Kevin Whelan for his advice and editorial involvement in the first edition, and to Nicholas Furlong, author and historian, for his encouragement and generousity in contributing the foreword to this book.

I

Rebellion:
26 May to 21 June 1798

It is said that the day on which the rebellion commenced was a beautiful warm and sunny afternoon in the rural village of The Harrow, in the parish of Boolavogue, a few miles to the north-east of the town of Enniscorthy. In the fields the barley crop was showing well and, from the hillside, the county of Wexford, with its well-tended farms and whitewashed thatched cottages, could be viewed spreading out to the west as far as the Blackstairs mountains, distantly shimmering in the heat of the afternoon sun. Only nature's sounds broke the silence, a bee droning from flower to flower in the headland or the urgent call of the blackbird to its mate. But on this Saturday, 26 May 1798, the idyllic calm of this pastoral setting would, by midnight, have changed to one of high activity and excitement, the urgent gathering of men and arms, meetings and preparations and the first shots would have been fired in a great and traumatic rebellion against the Crown in the south-east of Ireland.

It was not unexpected, though there was an element of chance in the how and where of its beginning. Tension had been growing in Ireland for years between the rulers and those they ruled, in a country where a small minority held all power and owned all the land, whilst giving allegiance to a different race, church, culture and language from those of the disenfranchised majority over whom they exerted power. The 'common people', the Catholic majority making up almost of 90 per cent of the population, had lived through almost a century of penal laws, which had virtually excluded them from all participation in the politics and commerce of the country. They could not purchase or own land, become members of parliament, join the professions or openly practice their religion without fear of persecution. Presbyterians, mainly living in the north eastern counties, were subject to similar, if somewhat less severe, restrictions.

Quite apart from their more recent treatment under early-eighteenth-century Acts, there was an abiding memory of previous wrongs festering in the hearts of those of the dispossessed Irish, as well as old English, inhabitants of the country who had adhered to Catholicism. Around winter firesides in Wexford, younger generations were reminded that their Murphy, Kinsella, Cavanagh, Doran, Browne, Roche or McMorrough forebears had, before confiscation and plantation, been the 'rightful' owners of the lands on which many of them now laboured as tenants. Though life went on through the years and decades, with crops sown and harvested, marriages made and children raised, a strong and persistent sense of injustice existed in the minds of the long-oppressed majority. Should the opportunity arise this was a recipe for rebellion.

Wexford is a maritime county which, in 1798, had two major ports in Wexford and New Ross. The constant comings and goings of ships to America and continental Europe, in the grain trade or, perhaps, to fish on the Newfoundland Banks, meant that many Wexford men regularly travelled abroad, or met with those who had, and people were fully aware of the great political changes which were occurring elsewhere in this Age of Enlightenment. The French Revolution, with its principles of liberty, equality and fraternity; the American War of Independence and the establishment of a republic promising freedom and equality before the law, and, of course, Tom Paine's espousing of the 'Rights of Man', were known and discussed. And so, when the Society of United Irishmen was founded in October 1791 proposing the establishment of a liberal and egalitarian regime of Catholic, Protestant and Dissenter, it found a ready acceptance by many Catholics and Presbyterians as well as a large number of liberal members of the Established Church. The existence of this society, which by 1798 had attracted hundreds of thousands of adherents, caused considerable concern to the government, particularly after a failed landing, organised by Theobald Wolfe Tone, by French troops in December, 1796.

By early 1798 the situation in County Wexford was, as in many other parts of the country, one of high activity and excitement. Pikes were being manufactured in large numbers and secret meetings were being held nightly to make revolutionary plans. Society was very much divided, not just between Catholic and Protestant, but with part of the Catholic side being strongly in favour of using only peaceful means of making progress and placing their trust in the power of persuasion, while, probably the majority of their fellows had had enough of injustice and oppression and were eager for the fight. The Catholic Bishop of Ferns, Dr Caulfield, was vehemently against any use of force and tried, through his priests, to dampen any inclination amongst his flock towards armed conflict, begging his people to hand in their arms to local magistrates. Whether he suspected it or not, however, a number of his priests were already members of the Society of United Irishmen and held a very different view of the politics of situation to that of their bishop.

There was also division in the Protestant camp, with a number of extreme individuals and groups bent on goading the people into rebellion, finally crushing all opposition and confirming their hold on authority. Against this, many liberal and more reasonable members of the Established Church sympathised deeply with the plight of their Catholic neighbours and favoured repeal and the establishment of a more generous form of government.

The activities of many of the local Orange Order and Yeomanry groups were excessive and making the work of the pacifists virtually impossible. Armed gangs and Yeomanry units were travelling about, particularly at night, threatening and beating at will, seeking information about local organisers of the United Irishmen, taking prisoners and burning family homes. Many rural families resorted by 'taking to the furze', and sleeping on the hillsides out of fear of these nightly visitations. As time went on, the floggings and pitchcappings[1] became more and more commonplace, as more than a hint of panic began to show in the attitude of the authorities. On 24 May thirty Catholic men, whose loyalty was suspect, were taken out on Dunlavin green, in County Wicklow, and shot. On the following day, at Carnew, on the Wexford/Wicklow border, twenty-eight prisoners, arrested on suspicion of being United Irishmen, were, on the order of the magistrate, taken to the local ball alley and executed.

By Saturday 26 May, County Wexford was buzzing with the news of rebel outbreaks in the north, as well as in Carlow and Kildare, and the outrageous response by the authorities in carrying out mass murders in order to terrorise the community. Yet there were many, concerned with the future of their families, and uncertain of the best course of action, who were still responding to the pleadings of their bishop by surrendering their arms at designated collection points, in return for a written guarantee of protection. This was, of course, a double-edged sword, for a weapon surrendered left the person who brought it in both without a means of defence as well as becoming a marked man, whose true loyalties were in doubt.

Fr John Murphy, the curate in the parish of Boolavogue, whatever his personal politics may have been, was a loyal and obedient servant of his bishop, Dr Caulfield, and, in response to the bishop's admonitions, had been seeking to persuade his flock that the best course of action was to surrender their arms. He was not a sworn member of the Society of United Irishmen, though, doubtlessly, he had been approached by them. In response to his pleadings a number of men of the parish decided to hand up their few guns and newly made pikes on that Saturday, at the residence of Lord Mountnorris. The curate later followed on, on horseback, only to meet his parishioners, having handed in their weapons, being chased by mounted local yeomanry, known as the 'black mob', firing their guns as they jeered at and harassed the unarmed men. For many of those in the parish who were undecided this was the final straw. Groups of men soon gathered around the district discussing the situation, the burnings of local houses, the awful news from Dunlavin and Carnew, their treatment that day by the local Yeomanry, and who was likely to be next on the list for capture, pitchcapping or imprisonment. Attitudes were quickly hardening in favour of action, with residual fear and apprehension being replaced by anger and determination. This was to be the evening that Fr John Murphy, curate in the parish of Boolavogue, changed from being a follower to a leader, when his first loyalty changed from being one of submission to orders of his bishop to becoming a decisive and effective rebel general at the head of his people. When the Camolin Yeoman Cavalry, under the command of Lt Bookey, set out, that evening, on a house raiding party, their direction had been closely observed and it was adjudged that they would return by way of a little village called The Harrow.

Under the command of the local curate an ambush was planned and, as they came into range Tom Donovan raised his gun and fired the first shot of the rebellion, killing his first cousin John Donovan, a member of the yeomanry. Leiutenent Bookey was piked from his horse as his cavalry fled down the hill in fright and incredulity. By their arrogant bullying and mistreatment of the people they had sown the wind and were now about to reap the whirlwind.

Nobody slept that night. Raiding parties were sent out seeking arms and to recover arms already surrendered, and men were called quickly together from the neighbouring parishes. It was not to be as the United Irishmen had planned it, but the rebellion had now begun and their detailed planning was now to be put to the test. Those in charge at Boolavogue – John Murphy, Tom Donovan and others – quickly set out to spread the word, and young nineteen-year-old Jerry Donovan was mounted on a pony, dressed in the uniform of a member of the yeomanry, and sent south to bring news to the parishes of Oulart, Blackwater and Castlebridge. There is still a strong and persistent folk memory, in places he passed, of him riding through the night shouting, 'It's on, get up and fight, get up and fight.' Alas, poor Jerry was himself killed fighting a few weeks later at the Battle of Arklow.

On the following day, Whit Sunday 27 May, came the first big test for both the rebels and authorities. By midday about 1,000 men had gathered on Oulart Hill, a few miles to the south of Boolavogue, poorly armed and, indeed, with some entirely unarmed, a number with fowling pieces or muskets but, mostly, holding only locally forged pikes, fitted with twelve-foot-long ash handles. That morning 200 of Hawtrey White's cavalry had left Gorey early and, on arrival, circled the foot of the hill, without taking any action. In Wexford town 150 members of the garrison of the North Cork Militiia made ready to leave about eleven o'clock to 'disperse' the crowd reported to have gathered some twelve miles north of the town.

Meanwhile the rebels had been augmented by the arrival of men from the northern area of the Maccamores, a number of them with fowling pieces and very skilled in their use. A plan was drawn up to lure the Redcoats into a trap by setting an ambush around a large field on the top of Oulart Hill, behind which the bulk of the men were placed. They were hidden behind the ditches on three sides, while another section showed themselves from behind the fourth boundary, facing the approach of the militia. As the Redcoats marched up the hill to the beat of the drum they did so with the confident assurance of trained professional soldiers, under the command of Maj. Lombard and Col. Foote. Some of those watching the orderly and controlled approach began to weaken in their resolve. A man named Morgan Byrne of Kilnamanagh, seeing some of his line wavering, ran behind shouting, 'Don't be afraid of their red coats, inside them they are just men like you, if you met them below at the fair in Ferns without their coats, would you fear them?'

When the militia reached the first ditch, those behind fired a few shots and turned to run as if in terror. The ruse worked and the soldiers charged after them, soon finding themselves under heavy attack from three sides. Then the pikemen came over the ditches and got in amongst them and within twenty minutes the rebels and their leaders had, in their first experience of major battle, proved themselves more than a match for the professional troops, fully equipped, as they were, and trained in the arts of war. The troops from Wexford town garrison lay, virtually wiped out, on the summit of Oulart Hill. Late in the afternoon, Col. Foot, together with a sergeant and three privates, made their way back across Wexford bridge to break the appalling news of their total and overwhelming defeat at the hands of the army of the people. As the enormity of their losses began to be realised, a sense of panic and foreboding quickly spread amongst the loyalist citizens of Wexford.

On the following day, the United Irish army was beginning to take on the look of an organised force and set about taking the town of Enniscorthy. Men were responding to the call from all the parishes, particularly those in central and northern parts of the county. Young John Kelly of Kilanne came marching into the vicinity Enniscorthy at the head of 600 men from Rathnure and the surrounding areas, while 'General' Thomas Cloney arrived at Davidstown crossroads with nearly as many from the barony of Bantry. The attack on that day, 28 May, was fiercely resisted and lasted for hours, before the rebels completed their victory, with the retreat of the Enniscorthy defenders towards Wexford.

Though they were to fight with great courage and determination, the eventual defeat of the United Irish army in County Wexford has been attributed mainly to three failings: shortages of materials, guns, powder and military equipment; inexperience on the part of their leadership and a lack of an overall and coherent strategy and contingency planning. Here, after the capture of Enniscorthy, the first signs of this inexperience began to show in the thinking of those in command. The whole central area of County Wexford was effectively under their control and they could have decided to next attack New Ross to the west, which was then, still lightly defended, thus taking control of the Barrow bridge and the route into Kilkenny and Munster. They still had the element of surprise and might have decided to march north, through Wicklow, gathering men along the way, attacking Dublin and making the movement of government troop reinforcements into County Wexford a far more difficult undertaking. Instead they opted for the most attractive prize, the county capital, the city of Wexford with its port and industry, lying only fourteen miles to the south. With hindsight, it would seem that, with Wexford town already cut off by land, the immediate capture of the lightly defended New Ross might have proved, in the longer term, far more enduringly advantageous.

The United army set out for Wexford and camped, on the evening of Tuesday 29 May, at Forth Mountain about three miles from the town. By now, having been joined by men pouring in from around the county, they had grown to a very considerable force, numbering about 10,000 in all, including camp followers. In Wexford Col. Maxwell was delaying in the hope of relief from Duncannon fort, having sent Mr John Sutton, earlier that day, to seek urgent reinforcements. Gen. Fawcett immediately set out to the relief of the town, with a force of 200 militiamen, to be followed, a little later, by 100 men of the Meath militia and a howitzer corps of the Royal Artillery. Fawcett decided to camp overnight at Taghmon and the second group pressed on for Wexford late on the night of the 29 May. When reports reached the insurgents of the immanent arrival of the relief column, an attack on them was assigned to the Bantry men, commanded by Thomas Cloney together with John Kelly of Kilanne. They assembled in the darkness on a steep hill beside the road, along which the Meath militia would pass, and the massed pikemen charged down upon them in a surprise attack. Within fifteen minutes the battle was over, the guns had been captured, together with the officer in charge and a number of gunners. Most of the Meath militia were killed but a small group escaped to return to Taghmon, where they informed Fawcett of the news. He immediately decided to withdraw back to the safety of Duncannon.

The following morning Maxwell, who had a defending force of some 700 men, decided to sally forth with a view to joining up with Fawcett, unaware of the most recent victory by the rebels, and was met with a number of shots from the captured howitzers. He quickly withdrew into the town and, while feigning discussions of terms, managed to escape, with all his force and equipment, by the southern road to Duncannon, leaving the town open to the United Irish army, which marched in to great rejoicing by all but the loyalist elite.

A meeting was arranged on the evening of 31 May, still recalled in Wexford as the 'big meeting', to take place in the largest public room in the town in Kenny's Hall,[2] at South Main street. It was in this place that the honourable principles and courageous determination to establish a worthy and just regime were clearly demonstrated by leaders of the people, still hot from the battles of the previous days. The French influence was obvious from the very beginning with individuals addressed as 'citizen' and a committee of public safety appointed. A Senate and a Grand Committee of 'leading men' from throughout the county was established and a Council of Elders, consisting of four Catholics and four Protestants, was put in place to take care of day to day affairs. Beauchamp Bagnal Harvey, a Protestant barrister, was made commander-in-chief of the army, John Howlin was appointed admiral of the navy (then consisting of four armed oyster boats), and Cornelius Grogan was a made chairman of the Commissariat, charged with providing food and supplies. Courts and judges were appointed, passes and ration licenses issued and Kenny's Hall was designated the Senate House. The first aim of the Society of United Irishmen had become a reality; the Wexford Republic had been put in place.

The new republic had little time to become established for, without good communications and intelligence, people were not aware of how the fight was going elsewhere in the country and did not yet realise that, beyond their county borders, the rising was already over or, effectively, lost. Very soon they would be alone in the fight and at the mercy of all the forces which the government could muster. In those early days of June the leaders were concerned with consolidating their position and bringing order and discipline to the army of the people. However, on 2 June Lord Kingsborough was arrested, when his ship was captured outside Wexford harbour, and with him came the first confirmation that things had gone badly for the United Irish challenge elsewhere in the country. The Wexford leadership now realised that their only hope was to spread the rebellion into Munster and northwards towards Dublin, and that the capture of New Ross and Arklow were now seen to be of paramount importance. The army was divided into two groups, the northern army, under Gen. Edward Roche, John Murphy, Edward Fitzgerald, Myles Byrne and others, taking up camp on Vinegar Hill, outside Enniscorthy, while the southern army, under Bagnal Harvey, Col. Cloney, Richard Monaghan and John Kelly camped on Carrigbyrne Hill, about six miles from New Ross. Harvey, though an honourable, committed and brave leader, was to prove, alas, to be vacillating and inept in command, and a poor choice for commander-in-chief. While he waited and dithered at Carrigbyrne the government were rushing reinforcements to New Ross, force marching troops from as far away as west Cork.

In the meantime the northern army had had, on 4 June, perhaps their most famous victory of the campaign, at Tubberneering, over an army of 1,800 troops, under the command of Gen. Loftus, which had left the Redcoats completely routed and in flight and their artillery captured.

Having spent four days at Carrigbyrne, Harvey, at last, moved with his army of about 12,000 men towards New Ross on the evening of 4 June 1798. In the town the defenders had greatly strengthened their perimeter and had some 2,000 regular troops, under the command of experienced Maj.-Gen. Henry Johnson, supported by yeomanry units as well as cannon. Confident in his strength of numbers, Harvey, early the following morning, sent an emissary, Matthew Furlong, under a flag of truce, to demand the surrender of the town. He was shot down from his horse in a hail of bullets and, immediately, the attack on the town commenced. The insurgents' plan of battle seems to have suffered greatly from a lack of cohesion and authority for, having fought bravely and attacked the town for hours and, indeed, come tantalizingly close to final success, the day ended with United Irish army retreating in some disorder, with many

Miles Byrne, from the north Wexford village of Monaseed, was one of the most brilliant and committed young leaders of the United Irish army in 1798. It was he who counselled that a surprise night attack should be mounted on the British camp, on the night before the Battle of Vinegar Hill, which would have helped offset the government forces' superiority in men and weapons. He escaped to Paris after the rebellion and joined the Irish Legion in the French army, with which he saw action before retiring, in 1834, with the rank of Chef-de-Bataillon. He is the only '98 man known to have been photographed and lived into old age in Paris. John Mitchell met him in the 1860s saying, 'walking on some of these bright winter days along the avenue of the Champs Elysees you may see a tall figure, the splendid ruin of a soldier *d'elite*, bearing himself, still erect, under the weight of eighty years.' He died in 1862 and is buried in Monmarte cemetery in Paris, where his grave is marked by a celtic cross. (Photograph reproduced by kind permission of Nicholas Furlong from his book *Fr John Murphy*.)

men leaving, disheartened, to return to their homes, and upward of a thousand of their comrades lying dead in the streets of the town.

Four days later, on Saturday 9 June, the northern army attacked Arklow and, after hard fighting in the town and running out of powder they, too, suffered defeat, losing somewhere between 500 and 1,000 men.

Despite these setbacks the Republic entered its third week still holding most of the county, though, by now, there must have been a growing realisation of the gathering strength of their foes, the increasing numbers of trained soldiers arriving to oppose, with almost infinite resources in the materials of war at their command. The tightening of the noose around the county of Wexford must have been having an effect on the confidence of many amongst both leaders and followers. And yet, in the main, though some gave up the fight and returned to homes and families, the vast majority were to hold bravely together to the bitter end. On 20 June, 6,000 rebels, lead by Philip Roche, fought a long and hard battle against forces under Gen. Sir John Moore, at Goff's Bridge, before retiring in good order.

On the following day, Thursday 21 June, the last great set piece battle on Irish soil was to decide the outcome of the United Irish challenge to the government and, though the numbers of about 25,000 on each side appear to give a semblance of balance to the engagement, the truth is that the overwhelming superiority of the British force left the outcome in little doubt. The brave young Miles Byrne had argued for a surprise attack by night, as a way to create some advantage to the rebels, but this was turned down. When the battle commenced it soon became clear that courage and pikes, together with a random collection of muskets and guns in the hands of brave young farmer's sons and farm labourers, carpenters, thatchers and smiths, were no match for a trained professional army supported by cavalry and artillery, using exploding shells for the first time in battle on an unsuspecting enemy. For many that day was to be the end, for others just the beginning of a long and determined resistance that would end far away from the smoke and clamour of Vinegar Hill.

Kenny's Hall, now occupied by Penney's stores, in South Main Street, Wexford, where the 'big meeting' was held on 31 May 1798 to establish the Wexford Republic. The meeting appointed senators; a Committee of Public Safety; a commander-in-chief, Bagnal Harvey; an admiral of the navy, John Scallan; a Commissariat under Cornelius Grogan, and a Council made up of four Protestants and four Catholics. The meeting hall, which became the Senate House until the rebellion was crushed, had, coincidentally, been the same building in which Cromwell had lodged in 'the panelled south west room on the second storey', when he occupied the town in 1649. The bronze plaque outside reads 'The Senate and Committee of Public Safety of the Wexford Republic convened here in June 1798'.

2

Uncertainty:
22 June to 5 July 1798

For many people the story of '98 ends with the Battle of Vinegar Hill and, in some senses, it does. The concentration of more than 25,000 troops in the county of Wexford, well armed and supplied, under the command of eight full generals and supported by artillery, effectively ended any possibility of a military victory by the determined and brave, but poorly equipped, insurgent army. With this defeat went all their hopes of a successful political revolution and the establishment of their own republic.

But this was not the end of the matter for the insurgents. Although they had suffered grievous casualties in the battle, most of the Wexford army made good their escape through Needham's Gap and camped, that night, in the woods of Sleedagh, below Wexford town. As if to show that their spirit was still unbroken, on the following day, Friday 22 June 1798, they performed a deed of quite extraordinary character. Setting out from Sleedagh at daybreak, they outflanked the Government army and, by nightfall, 5,000 men had safely passed through the Scullogue Gap into County Carlow, having marched a distance of more than forty miles.

Led by Fr John Murphy, their plan was to move into Laoise and Kilkenny, where it was hoped to raise support, and then extend the struggle into the midland counties. On the morning of 23 June they attacked the garrison at Goresbridge, in County Carlow, made up of the Wexford Town Militia and the Fourth Dragoon Guards. After a short but fierce engagement, the defenders, many of whom were Wexford townsmen and personally known to their attackers, surrendered, although a number managed to make good their escape.

That night the insurgents moved on and camped on the Ridge of Leinster, at Baunreagh. Between them and the planned route north, lay the town of Castlecomer, then defended by a force of about 500 men. Gen. Asgill, realising the importance of denying Castlecomer to the rebels, set out from Kilkenny with almost 1,000 men, early that morning, and arrived in time to observe the battle already joined in various locations around the town. Miles Byrne was to the fore in leading the attack and Asgill, judging that the town was already effectively lost, withdrew his troops to Kilkenny, declining to become involved.

The Wexford army, having completed their capture of the town, with the loss of about 100 men on their side, immediately moved on northwards towards Athy. Their route was through Moneenroe and, late that evening, 24 June, weary after the long day's fighting and marching, they crossed the River Deen into County Laoise, and camped on Keeffe's Hill, in the townland of Slatt.

We can never know the nature of the discussions which took place that night around the campfires on that hill in County Laoise but, despite their successes in recent battles, the feeling amongst the leadership seems too have been one of despondency. Riders, who had been sent ahead to scout the area, were reporting no signs of enthusiasm for joining with the rebels by the people of the district; rather there was a dread of what consequences might result from demonstrating any kind of association with them. Whilst their suffering and disaffection with the government may have equalled that of the Wexford men, they clearly had no appetite for open rebellion. In Wexford folk memory it is recalled that people they met 'were too frightened to pass the time of day or, even, to give them directions'. A decision was made that night to immediately march back to their native county and to accept whatever consequences might result, be it to fight on or seek to quietly disperse and individually return to what might remain of their homes.

They were to return, alas, without their courageous, dynamic and beloved leader. Having camped that night on Kilcumney Hill, the men set out next morning, under the command of Richard Monaghan and Miles Byrne. Fr John Murphy left camp a little later, by which time a dense fog had rolled down from the mountains, and he failed to make contact with the main group, who were making their way across the Blackstairs, through Cromwell Gap, and into County Wexford. He and his faithful friend and aide, James Gallagher, who had remained by his side throughout the rebellion, were later captured at O'Toole's Farm at Castlemore and put to death by the yeomanry at Tullow.[1]

On reaching the boundary of County Wexford the insurgents divided, some, under the command of Fr Mogue Kearns, moving to Killoughrim woods, while the main group, led by Miles Byrne, set out north-east towards the Wicklow border. This latter group joined up with a large force that had marched there from Wexford town, following its surrender on the previous week, and which was commanded by Anthony Perry, Edward Fitzgerald and Edward Roche. Together they would have made up a very considerable force – possibly numbering, in all, between 6,000 and 7,000 men, even when allowing for losses and defections, as many must have already decided that the game was lost, they could give no more, and set out for their homes.

By now, the entire county was effectively under the control of government forces, commanded by Generals Lake and Moore, and Lake's soldiers seem to have been given free rein to exact the most cruel vengeance on the general population. From the heights of the Blackstairs smoke could be seen rising the length of the county from Croghan Kinsella to Carnsore, as humble cottages were put to the torch and, by night, the darkness was everywhere broken by the glowing embers of thatch.

In Wexford many captured insurgents had been summarily tried and hanged on Wexford bridge, including young John Kelly of Kilanne and seventy-four-year-old Cornelius Grogan, who, ironically, had been one of the prime movers and shareholders when the same bridge was built by the American, Lemuel Cox, a few years earlier.

At this stage a great degree of uncertainty existed amongst the leadership as to what they should do next. Their original strategy of taking control of County Wexford and moving into surrounding counties as they rose had now failed, and government forces were now strengthening their position by the day. Any examination of the movements of the Wexford army from 26 June to 5 July makes it abundantly clear that they were operating without any coherent plan or purpose, marching and countermarching and attacking random targets as opportunities arose. This is not to say that there was any significant weakening in the commitment or morale of those who remained with the rebel army. The single constant throughout the campaign was the courage which the Wexford men were to display right to the end, and which was never disputed by friend or foe. Lake's biographer, Col. Pearse,[2] acknowledged that the Wexford men showed great gallantry and determination throughout and, while the rebels were to be demonised afterwards in some quarters, the professional soldiers against whom they had fought recalled them as courageous and unyielding foes. Gen. Sir John Moore, kindly remembered in Wexford, went as far as to say that, were he to have been forced to live under such conditions as they, he would have been amongst them, carrying his pike, in the streets of New Ross.

Despite their lack of any overall plan, the insurgents remained a formidable force and were still to have a degree of military success.

The contingent under Perry had left Wexford town and marched east, through Peppard's Castle and Gorey to Croghan Hill, where they remained until the morning of 25 June. They left here to march to Hacketstown and, defeating a party of yeomanry *en route*, attempted to storm the barracks in the town. Here they made a tactical blunder, which they were to repeat again, of attacking strong, well fortified, buildings without the aid of cannon or storming equipment of any kind, relying mainly on the cover of horse carts pushed ahead of the advancing men. Though they fought with great courage, they failed to breach the fortifications and lost many brave men in the attempt. Amongst those killed was young James Murphy, nephew of Fr Micheal Murphy – himself killed at the Battle of Arklow. At Hacketstown, where the rebels had not a single piece of artillery, they were led by Edward Fitzgerald, Anthony Perry, Garrett Byrne and Michael Reynolds (the latter losing his life in the course of the attack).

In the late afternoon the attack was broken off and the rebels withdrew to the east and the main body returned to Croghan Hill where they camped undisturbed on 27 and 28 June. After discussion amongst their leaders it was decided to make an attack on Carnew. There were three principal reasons behind this decision: first the intention was to seek to augment their limited supplies of powder and ammunition: second they were concerned at remaining too long at Croghan and thus creating an opportunity for a concerted attack by government forces; finally, the leadership's concern must have been to take any action at all rather than appearing to be, entirely, without purpose or plan.

Early on the morning of 29 June the rebel army marched through Monaseed, heading towards Carnew. They were pursued along their line of march by the cavalry corps of the Ancient Britons, together with several corps of yeomanry. The Wexford men turned to face them at Ballyellis, about a mile from Carnew, having first prepared an ambush along the approach road.

Over confident by virtue of recent successes, the Ancient Britons fell into the trap. After a battle of no more than half an hour's duration, the cavalry corps, together with many of their yeoman allies, had been overwhelmed, suffering great losses. On the following day a detachment of military and yeomanry, moving with caution towards Ballyellis, reported that the rebels had moved on. They brought back those bodies which they found and reported, as still missing, 25 Ancient Britons, 11 Fifth Dragoon Guards, 6 Gorey Cavalry and 2 Ballakeen Cavalry.

Meanwhile at Carnew the insurgents had, once again, made the cardinal error of attempting to take a strongly built and well garrisoned building without the aid of cannon and, having lost many men in the futile attempt to do so, withdrew to Kilcavan Hill, where they camped. Here they remained until Sunday morning, 1 July, when they marched on to Ballyraheen Hill, beyond Shillelagh.

Over the following days the insurgents sought to find a course of action which might give them some advantage in an uncertain situation. Generals Needham, Huntley and Duff were manoeuvring to trap them, though their constant mobility made this more difficult for the generals to achieve. Indeed, on the evening of 2 July, the government forces were baffled regarding the exact whereabouts of the main body of the insurgent army. Yet the government's grip on the situation was tightening perceptibly and the rebel positions were becoming increasingly unsustainable.

On the morning of Thursday 5 July, the Wexford army fought its last major battle on the soil of their native county at Ballygullen, north of Craanford. Here they met with an army group, numbering 1,000, with artillery and cavalry, under the command of Gen. Duff. The rebels inflicted a major defeat on the cavalry, but the battle ended in stalemate with many casualties on each side. The Wexford men, learning of the imminent arrival of reinforcements, under Gen. Needham, made a tactical withdrawal to avoid being encircled. That night the rebels marched back to their old camp at Carraigrue and it was here that the decision was made to move quickly into County Wicklow.

This move was tactically wise. In most of Wexford their position had become untenable in military terms while, in the mountains of Wicklow – difficult terrain for cavalry and the transport of artillery – they might find it possible to continue their resistance.

The principal leaders at Carraigrue were Anthony Perry, who had fought as a colonel in the British army during the American War of Independence, Mogue

Kearns, Esmond Kyan and Garret Byrne of Ballymanus. Three days earlier, on 2 July, Holt – the Wicklow leader – had left, together with 1,060 of his men and marched on through Ballymanus, Ballycurragh, Aughavanna, Glenmalure and Knockalt to Whelp Rock, above Black Hill and to the east of Blessington. The decision at Carraigrue was that the Wexford army should march on immediately and join him there.

Sometime, late on the night of 5 July, or very early on the following morning, the Wexfordmen left Carraigrue and, before dawn, had crossed over the county border into Wicklow. For a great many of them it was to be the last time they would ever see their native Wexford, for although they would not have known it then, they were setting out on a long march that was to bring them to the borders of County Cavan, far to the north.

3

Decision at Whelp Rock:
6 July to 9 July 1798

The camp at Whelp Rock was on the northern slopes of Black Hill, which rises to a height of 1,985ft above what is now Poulaphouca reservoir, although the water level of the lough was much lower in 1798.

It was a good defensive position, difficult to surround or on which to mount a surprise attack. Joseph Holt had been sent a dispatch from Carraigrue informing him that the main body of the Wexford army was on the march and that he could expect a force of 11,000 men. In his memoirs Holt says, 'Supposing that, as usual, they would not be overly well fed it became necessary for me to make provision for so numerous a company of visitors, and I determined not to be niggardly in hospitality.'[1]

In order to make such provision he commandeered two large boilers from Mr Radcliffe's factory at Ballynahown each of which, it was found, could take 6 cwt. of beef for cooking. The cooked beef was distributed to the men in turf kishes while the 'excellent' soup was stored in tubs. Despite these arrangements, one of the reasons contributing to their, eventually, moving from Whelp Rock was that the area was too desolate to support a large population of rebels, together with their animals.

According to both Holt and Miles Byrne the rebels arrived at Whelp Rock late on Thursday 5 July,[2] but they would seem have been in error here – one, perhaps, taking his lead from the other. There is certainly some doubt about the matter, and it would seem certain that they did not reach the camp until the following night, 6 Friday.

There is also a very great disparity between the accounts of the strength of the rebel army which arrived at the camp. One contemporary account stated that, 'they were about one thousand', while Holt, himself, with great precision, asserted that, on 9 July, 13,780 men had mustered at Whelp Rock.[3] However these figures were arrived at, in the light of subsequent events both figures would seem far off the mark. Allowing for the fact that Holt mentions that some 2,500 fewer marched on to Timahoe and that many, if not most, of the Wicklow men opted to return to Glenmalure, his figures would seem still on the high side; the figure of 1,000, on the other hand, is very much below the number that can be accounted for in the days that followed. Aylmer's recollection of having been joined in county Kildare by 4,000 men from Wicklow is reasonably accurate.

Quite apart from Holt's efforts in providing hospitality for his 'guests', the camp must have been fairly well organised and run. According to a statement by Daniel Doyne, while under examination after his capture, gunpowder and shot were being manufactured there. The spring and summer had been very fine, with no rain falling for several weeks, as a result of which the living conditions of the men on the open hillside could not have been too uncomfortable. Over the next couple of days, after their arrival, the leaders held a Council of War to decide what course of action they should follow.

According to the statement of Stephen Murray, a rebel from near Gorey, made under examination after his capture, 'at Whelp Rock the general of the whole was Esmond Kane (Kyan), a man who wanted the use of one hand.'[3]. Apart from Kyan, some of the others taking part in this important meeting were: Edward Fitzgerald of Newpark, Thomas Dixon of Castlebridge – a publican related by marriage to 'General' Roche, Garrett Byrne, Anthony Perry, Mogue Kearns and Holt. A further eighteen took part in the council, making a total of twenty-five in all, but the names of the others are no longer known to us with certainty. The meeting was a long and acrimonious one, which was to result, long afterwards, in recriminations and self-justification by some of those who were to survive the rebellion.

There were four possible courses of action to be discussed and which the leadership might have pursued:

1. Remain at Whelp Rock and seek to hold out as long as possible and until conditions might change in their favour, or when they might seek favourable terms from the government.
2. The army might be ordered to disband, allowing the men to make their way back to their homes and whatever fate might await them.
   (These first two strategies do not seem to have been deemed worthy of much debate and there is no indication from any of those involved that any inclination towards a surrender mentality existed within the leadership of the army).
3. A plan put forward and strongly argued for by Holt, together with a number of others. Holt proposed that the rebels should march across the mountains, perhaps by night, and make a surprise attack on Newtownmountkennedy. He had intelligence that there were two field pieces there, together with plenty of ammunition, 'which we could easily make ourselves master of'.[5] He then wanted to march the few miles south to Wicklow town, to release the large number of prisoners held there and turn quickly north to march on Dublin. This plan seems to have had much to recommend it, given the benefit of hindsight.

A great proportion of the government troops were still held in Wexford and south Wicklow and, had Holt's plan been attempted, it would have allowed the insurgents to outflank the main body of the enemy.

4. Mogue Kearns proposal that the army should immediately march through Kildare, join with Aylmer's group at Timahoe, and attack across the Boyne towards Athlone. Kearns argued strongly that a great many recruits would join the cause in the midland counties and that he had good knowledge of the region and many contacts there. Those against the plan pointed out that the conditions on the central plain would greatly favour the movement of troops and artillery by the government side, and be much more advantageous to the enemy cavalry.

The latter seems to have been a far less well considered option than that put forward by Holt, relying heavily on Kearns' belief that he would be able to motivate great numbers of people in the midlands to rally to his cause, and without nearly the same degree of detailed planning and certainty of purpose which Holt's plan contained. Kearns, however, was very forceful in his manner with a very strong personality and, amongst the leadership and men, undoubtedly gained great influence by virtue of his priesthood.

After much debate, it was finally decided to put the two options to a vote which Kearns narrowly won. According to Holt himself, 'it went to a poll and a majority of two decided in favour of Fr. Kearns'.[6]

The die was cast and the decision was to prove a fateful one. Afterwards many were to wonder at the decision. In his memoirs Miles Byrne muses, 'I could never learn the real motive which induced these leaders to quit the Wicklow mountains and march the Wexford Division, which had fought so gallantly and in so many battles, into open country like Kildare, Meath, Louth etc.'[7]

Holt is in no doubt. He lays the entire blame squarely on the shoulders of Kearns and is scathing on how the decision was made:

We left a strong country where we could have made good resistance and obtained terms, and moved into an open one apparently for the express purpose of delivering ourselves into our enemy's power. We were defeated, multitudes destroyed, taken and gibbeted; the folly of our acts brought its just punishment. To have proposed prudent measures previous to our advance on the Boyne; it would have produced certain death to anyone. Fr. Kearns, who had most influence over the Wexford fugitives, having suggested that measure, and although I said it folly, and tried to prevent it, the holy father was, from his sanctity of chance there, too much for me, and I was outvoted.

The priest could not err and many thousand poor devils fell victim to their confidence in the sanctified sagacity of their spiritual guide, but in military affairs they were worse than fools. Had I been in command of the rebel army before they left Whelp Rock for the Boyne, I would have made a dart at Newtown Mount Kennedy and do not doubt I should have succeeded in capturing the guns and ammunition there.[8]

Holt was not one of Kearns' most ardent admirers. Others were equally opposed to the plan to march through Kildare. Amongst the Wexford leaders, Edward Fitzgerald supported Holt's proposal and, in the days that were to follow, the consequences of the decision must have had some effect on the unity of purpose of those in command. From this point on Kearns, and his friend, Anthony Perry, made the important army decisions, even though no record remains which would indicate that they had assumed overall leadership. There is little doubt of Kearns' unquestioned authority after this point. Fintan Aylmer, writing only a few days later, on 16 July 1798, states, 'Kearns --- headed the party of rebels at Clonard'[9] and others also confirm this new leadership position which the priest had taken.

At the camp, once the decision was made, preparations were put in hand to march. Cattle were collected for driving ahead, cooking pots and other equipment gathered and packed up. Those with horses carried a pillion passenger, who exchanged places with those on foot at intervals, after which the horses were rested. Most of the rebels were without horses and carried their weapons and whatever little personal supplies they had. At eleven o'clock on the night of Monday 9 July, the Wexford army decamped and moved off from Whelp Rock.

Black Mountain and Whelp Rock viewed from Poulaphouca Lake.

A closer view of Whelp Rock, showing its inhospitable nature.

4

The Plains of Kildare:
9 July to 11 July 1798

The rebel army marched through Blessington and down to Kilcullen and, skirting Newbridge at a brisk pace, across the flat plains of the Curragh. They passed through Robertstown and on to the vicinity of Prosperous, where they briefly camped. At some time, late in the evening of 10 July, they arrived at the camp of the Kildare United men at Timahoe. The camp was on a slight rise of ground in the Bog of Allen and, in command of the Kildaremen, was William Aylmer of Painstown together with other local leaders Luby and Ware.[1] Kildare had been a strong centre of the United Irishmen, with a registered membership of 12,703 in 1797, and had played a major role in the rebellion before the arrival of the Wexfordmen.[2] Aylmer had fought well at battles at Maynooth, Clane and Kilcock but, following initial successes, thing had begun to go wrong. At Ovidstown, on 20 June, they had been severely defeated, with the loss of over 200.

Initially there had been four camps in the county, at Knockallen Hill, Gibbet Hill, near to the Curragh, Blackmore Hall, near the Wicklow border, and Timahoe. The Blackmore Hall and Gibbet Hill men had surrendered and disbanded, perhaps on terms locally agreed. At the time of the arrival of the Wexford rebels only Timahoe remained, with a compliment of about 15,000 men.

Aylmer had judged that the cause was, by now, hopeless and was in the process of suing for terms. On 20 June, nearly three weeks previously, he had written a letter to his father asking him to arrange a truce through the Marquis of Buckingham, with whom his father was friendly. He, in turn, made contact with Cornwallis and peace negotiations were put in train.[3]

The arrival of the Wexfordmen, still full of spirit and keen to fight on, was not likely to have been welcomed by the Kildare leadership, already in the middle of peace talks. Furthermore, the strategy proposed by the Wexford leadership did not impress them. They would have been in a better position to judge the temper of those whom Kearns hoped to attract to his cause at this late stage in the rebellion, as well as being more aware of local conditions, and must have thought the Wexford plan quite impracticable. The fact that Aylmer expressed surprise at the shortages of supplies and ammunition in the ranks of the army, which had just arrived, can not have added much to his confidence in their ability to continue with the war against an enemy which was becoming stronger and more attentive by the day.[4]

So, while we can imagine Kearns arguing, in his very forceful way, that the two forces join together and march on, the appeal failed to move the Kildare leaders from their plan to seek terms and rescue whatever they might from impending defeat. Much has been made of the failure of the Timahoe men to give support to the Wexford army, but a great deal of the immediate criticism made, perhaps in the suffering and anger of defeat, is not entirely justifiable.

In his *History of Ireland* Revd James Gordan says, 'The fierce Wexfordians pursued, unaided, their plan of desperate adventure; finally separating from their less enterprising associates, against whom, in consequence of some disputes, they had, with difficulty, been prevented from turning their arms.'

In his *Insurrection of '98* Revd Patrick Kavanagh's comment, in relation to the battle of 11 July is, 'This repulse the Wexfordmen attribute to the cowardice of their Kildare associates, who neither aided them in the attack on Tyrrell's house, nor joined them in resisting the troops.'

Seen, however, in the light of the decision of Aylmer and his men to sue for terms, before the arrival of the insurgents from Wexford, and his obvious doubts regarding the merits of their plan, it seems churlish to attribute their failure to co-operate to any lack of courage on the part of the Kildare rebels. Edward Fitzgerald, together, perhaps, with many of his personal followers, remained behind in Timahoe, when the Wexford army left the following morning.

There are some reports which refer to Fitzgerald being with the rebel army later than 11 July, but these are far less convincing than the clear evidence that he remained behind. Miles Byrne mentions, 'the main body commanded by Fitzgerald, Garrett Byrne, Kearns, Esmond Kyan etc., which had marched into the counties Meath, Louth and Dublin' but gives no details of the duration of their involvement. Indeed, in accounts of this final part of the campaign, memoirs often written long afterwards are sometimes uncertain about who was exactly where and when. A further intelligence report refers to Fitzgerald having addressed the rebels at Ballyboughill – after he had, already, surrendered to the government. In this instance it is clear that the report erred in mistaking him for Esmond Kyan, who was the acknowledged leader at that time.

Fitzgerald had the same pragmatic view as that of Aylmer; he had been against leaving Whelp Rock, and had little faith in their proposed course of action. He participated in negotiating a truce, together with Alymer, and met with Gen. Wilford for this purpose at Sallins. He was one of the seventeen who subsequently signed the truce at Rathcoffey and surrendered himself, with the Kildaremen, on 21 July. It does not seem likely, or possible, for him to have marched on with the insurgents in these circumstances but, rather, that he decided at Timahoe that no useful purpose might be served by continuing the fight.

The only argument, perhaps, which might be made for his having gone on as far as Clonard, before, immediately, returning to Timahoe, is that there is no record of dissention in the Wexford camp which would have, almost certainly, occurred had there been any split in the leadership at Timahoe. There appears to have been total unity of purpose, from what is known, as almost the entire body prepared to move on – even gaining a few allies from the ranks of the Kildaremen.

For some unexplained reason there was a delay in moving out of camp on the morning of Wednesday 11 July, and the army did not get on the road until about nine o'clock. Then, together with their leaders, Kearns, Perry, Holt, Kyan and Garrett Byrne, the Wexfordmen set off north-west towards the coach road and Clonard.

Timahoe. The precise camp location is uncertain but the area shown here was, very probably, part of the site.

Rathcoffey House, now ruined, where Aylmer and Fitzgerald negotiated terms for surrender.

The bridge over the Grand Canal at Robertstown, Co. Kildare, over which the Wexford insurgents passed late in the evening of 10 July 1798, on their march to Alymer's camp at Timahoe.

5

Clonard:
11 July 1798

The historic little village of Clonard lies astride the N4, linking Dublin with the west, in a corner of County Meath, bordering closely on the adjoining counties of Westmeath, Kildare and Offaly. It is an old and important centre, mentioned in many of the Annals, and was the site of a monastery and school, founded by St Finian in the year 513. Less than a mile to the east is the Leinster Bridge, which spans the Boyne and marks the border with County Kildare. Built in 1831, the present bridge replaced an older structure, which was sited about 100 yards further upstream and which formed part of the old coach road from the capital to Mullingar, Athlone and Galway.

In 1798, this was a toll bridge and the approach, on the Dublin side, was blocked by two large, heavy, iron gates in the immediate vicinity of the toll house. An old toll house is still standing, at the time of writing, but this is not the same building which served in 1798.

There were a number of other buildings, including a dozen or so thatched cottages, near to the bridge, all of which have disappeared, leaving only remnants of their outline; a few mounds of rubble and an occasional piece of cut stone. On the Meath side of the bridge there was a coaching inn which boasted, 'Good dry lodgings and breakfast by Hugh Ennis, Clonard',[1] together with a coach yard. The most imposing building, standing on the Kildare side, was the substantial stone house, owned by John Tyrrell.

Tyrrell was a member of an old established and important family, which had a number of branches in the area. The Tyrrells were one of the earliest Anglo-Norman families to settle in Ireland and had, for centuries, been active in the commerce and politics of the country, giving their name to the town of Tyrrellspass. They had been particularly active, on the Irish side, during the O'Neill rebellions of the seventeenth century. John Tyrrell, the owner of the house at Leinster Bridge, was a kinsman of

Thomas Tyrrell, then High Sheriff of County Kildare, and, in those early months of 1798 he had gone to England – it was said on business.

Some time in March or April of that year, Thomas Tyrrell became concerned at the developing political situation and set about taking what precautionary measures he could. Recognising that his own house at Kilriney, near Clonard, was difficult to defend and fearing, with some justification, that he would be a marked man in the event of hostilities breaking out, he moved, together with his wife and family, into the house of John Tyrrell at Leinster Bridge. He would also have been aware of the strategic importance of the Boyne Bridge and so he placed a corps of cavalry on permanent duty at Clonard. He also set about fortifying the house, which was of solid stone construction, by building up the lower windows and doors with masonry. One important feature was a tower or turret of some kind, built on the grounds near the main house. This structure was in a commanding position, in view of the bridge, and was to play a crucial part in the events to follow. The grounds were either entirely or substantially enclosed by a stone wall, which added further to the security of the building.

On the outbreak of hostilities in County Kildare, the High Sheriff travelled to Dublin and pleaded with Lord Castlerea to send down a corps of regular troops. His request was denied but he was promised ample supplies of arms and ammunition for any further yeomanry he might be able to enlist.

Sometime in the morning of 11 July, Richard Allen of Ballinlig, a nephew of Thomas Tyrrell, galloped into the yard shouting that the United men were coming down the coach road. It must have been about nine o'clock, as the garrison had good time to make preparations for an attack. According to local tradition, an old and infirm member of the family, possibly the father of John or Thomas Tyrrell, was carried out of the house and taken some distance away to safety. The road gates near the bridge were closed and locked and a rider, possibly the same Richard Allen who had brought the news, rode away towards Kinnegad and Mullingar to raise the alarm and seek reinforcements.

Many varying estimates are given of the strength of the insurgent army at this time. In an account given in the appendix to Kavanagh a figure of 10,000 is mentioned, while Maxwell, in his *History of the Irish Rebellion*, asserts that they numbered 4,000. Gordan states that there were 1,500. Both of the first two figures would seem to be exaggerated – the first wildly so. Most historians, and local tradition, suggest that the army marching towards Clonard consisted of some 2,000 to 2,500 active fighting men. They were almost all Wexfordmen, with smaller contingents from south and west Wicklow and included a group of men from Kildare, who continued on the march, despite what differences they may have had. That they were led by Perry and Kearns is beyond doubt. In a letter dated Monday 16 July, only five days after the event, Fintan Aylmer, writing to Lord Castlerea from Maynooth, says, 'Kearns, a Wicklow or Wexford priest, headed the party of rebels at Clonard, a very tall able man.'[2]

They are remembered in local tradition as having looked bedraggled, with many of their number dressed in torn and dirty clothing. This is hardly surprising when we consider that they were men who had been marching and fighting constantly for weeks on end, sleeping rough when they could, hungry and tired and ever being harassed by their enemy. It is a matter of great wonder that so many remained loyal and spirited having suffered such hardship. As Miles Byrne recorded, 'Such tenacity, despite weary marching, and lack of food and ammunition, is truly amazing'.

They were mostly on foot but, as Willie Beatty of Ballindoolin states, 'they had a good deal of horses with them'. The garrison of Tyrrell's house numbered only about forty, including eighteen soldiers under a sergeant, Tyrrell himself and his family, and the Clonard yeomanry under the command of Lt Barlow, commanding in the absence of John Tyrrell, who was their captain. Tyrrell placed his six best riflemen in the tower overlooking the approach road.

On first sight the odds seem overwhelming – 2,500 against 40 – with a quick victory assured for the insurgent forces, but this was not at all the case: in fact the opposite was true. The defenders were in the protection of a solid stone building, which had been specially fortified so as to make it virtually impregnable against a lightly armed attack. They were well armed and supplied with ammunition. Facing them were forces mainly armed with pikes and some light arms who had to attack over open ground, and who were without cannon or other means of enfilading the house. In the circumstances numbers were of no advantage but, rather, provided a bigger target for those firing on them from the upper windows and slit openings left in the walls.

The difficulty of mounting a successful attack in the circumstances was recognised by the leaders of the Wexfordmen; they had experienced this problem many times before, and more that one commentator mentions that the insurgents might have passed on without doing so but for fire being opened on them as they approached the bridge. One of their number, a man named Willie Farrell, approached the house on horseback and was shot dead by young Thomas Tyrrell, the seventeen-year-old second son of John Tyrrell. The killing of Farrell, who has been referred to as 'Captain' Farrell and was clearly a leader at some level, angered the insurgents and they rushed the house suffering a great many casualties – particularly from the fire of the party in the high tower. Maxwell's version of the event is slightly different. He says:

> The rebel cavalry, amounting in rough numbers to three hundred, formed an advance guard and were commanded by a man named Farrall. Unconscious that the garden turret was occupied, they came forward in a trot, and the first intimation that they were already under fire was conveyed by a shot from the youngest Tyrrell – a boy only fifteen years old – which mortally wounded the rebel captain. A volley from the other loyalists emptied several rebel saddles; a panic ensued and the horsemen galloped out of musket range, leaving several of their companions dead on the road.

The difficulty of the problem was now clear to the insurgent leaders, if there had been any doubt before. The house was impossible to approach without loss of life. Tyrrell's best marksmen held commanding positions in the tower and upper windows of the manor house but, without controlling the house, they could not cross the bridge.

A large group was sent up behind the opposite ditch, using the hedge for cover, and opened fire on the turret but without having any effect on the defenders. At the same time the main force sought to surround the house but, while they had no difficulty on the main approaches, they could not complete their encirclement without holding the bridge. A group was then sent onto the bridge, but found itself in a direct line of fire from the house, and about ten men were killed in the first fusillade, forcing them to abandon their positions. Thus the garrison and their means of communication with the western side of the river remained intact, as did access to the house by any relieving party.

Maxwell, in his version of the events, gives a backhanded compliment to the courage of the attackers when he reports 'In the first two attempts the insurgents were heavily repulsed – but defeat seemed only to exasperate them and they again came forward into the attack'.

Eventually they broke through the garden and into the lower portion of the tower. There were no stairs, access to the upper storey being by an opening in the ceiling, and the ladder had been drawn up. Climbing on each others shoulders they attempted to break through the trapdoor but each who tried was, in turn, killed. Those below then attempted to fire through the ceiling and thrust their long-handled pikes upwards in a vain attempt to dislodge their tormentors, but without success. Fire from above was deadly and accurate and twenty seven of the insurgents were killed inside the tower. A quantity of straw was then thrown in and set alight and soon the whole structure caught fire. The six musketeers in the tower were trapped by the flames beneath and two of them perished, but the other four contrived to jump into the hay yard from the upper window and, under cover of the smoke and protected by the garden wall, managed to run to the main house.

The nearby thatched houses soon caught fire, burning the bodies of a number of the Wexfordmen who had been removed there from the field of battle. It is probable that the original toll house was also burned down at this time.

The battle had been raging for six hours and the garrison had not been dislodged when, about five o'clock in the afternoon, reinforcements of yeomanry were seen coming from the direction of Kinnegad. They were not great in number – fourteen of the Kinnegad infantry, under the command of Lt Haughton, together with a sergeant and eleven Northumberland Fencibles. The Kinnegad contingent included local landlords Coppertwhaite and Rochford. Their arrival, however, signalled the end of the battle but, hardly, in the way later claimed by the yeomanry, who had it understood that they had routed the rebels. Such was their confidence, indeed, that they, afterwards, had their victory commemorated with a double jig entitled 'The Kinnegad Slashers'.

Arriving in time only to fire a few volleys, they crossed the bridge and joined the garrison in the house, just as the Wexfordmen had begun, what seems to have been, an orderly retreat. There is a suggestion that the rebels had run out of ammunition, which might well have been the case, but it would seem more likely, given subsequent events, that they felt the situation futile and wasteful of the little ammunition they had left, and decided to withdraw. In any event, it would seem that they had learned from bitter experience the folly of persisting in attacking what was, in effect, a fortress, at very great loss of life and with little hope of early success, and had decided on disengagement. In reality, it would seem very unlikely that men who had charged Walpole's Redcoats at Tubberneering, fought doggedly in the streets at New Ross, and men hardened by the heat of a score of battles, would have been panicked by the arrival of fourteen members of the local yeomanry from Kinnegad.

Disengagement from such a situation as this presents difficulties for even professionally trained armies and the rebels, including a great number armed only with pikes, might certainly, have given the impression of being in some disarray, as could have been expected. During their retreat from the immediate area of the house the insurgents were harassed by the yeomanry and the Northumberland Fencibles but, though they, undoubtedly, suffered further losses, there was no semblance of panic in their withdrawal and march on to Carbery, or Castlecarbery as it was then called.

The yeomanry had, however, achieved one small, though significant, success by capturing, as a trophy, the banner of the Whitechurch insurgents. The triangular pennant, bearing the harp and the legend 'God Save Ireland', together with the placename 'Whitechurch', was in the possession of Mr Jasper Tyrrell of Ballinderry House, Carbery, until very recently. There is some question about the authenticity of the flag and it has been suggested that it may be a nineteenth-century copy of the original.

While they had not been routed as such, the battle was, nevertheless, something of a disaster for the men of Wexford. They had failed to take their objective and had suffered grievous losses in their attempt. In the region of 160 had been killed and 60 wounded, while their enemy had suffered only a few casualties – two killed, George Tyrrell and Michael Cusack, and three wounded, Richard Allen (who died later of his wounds), James Tyrrell and James Fairburn. It is a measure of the adequacy with which the loyalists were supplied that, during the battle, it is reported that the defenders had discharged more than 100 rounds per man.[3] It must be fully acknowledged, however, that one of the principle reasons for the insurgent's failure to take the house was the courageous and determined defence put up by the small garrison. Made up of the extended Tyrrell family and neighbours together with about twenty soldiers, to those inside the house the arrival of such a huge number of rebels to surround and attack the building must have presented a fearsome and daunting sight. Yet they showed a steely determination throughout the battle in continuing to fight, at no time giving any indication that they contemplated surrender.

In the aftermath of the battle the yeomanry rode throughout the area seeking rebels who had been separated from the main group, or who lay wounded, and treated them cruelly. Some of the dead were buried in a mass grave in a field near the banks of the Boyne, which was walled in, in 1873, by the owner, Garrett Robinson, and a memorial was erected there in 1898 by the people of the parishes of Ballyna, Kinnegad and Ballinabrackey.[4] The names of the sixteen Wexfordmen inscribed there are:

Dowd
Kiernan
Rochford
Sinnott

Doyle
Redmond
Roach[5]
Boland
Reilly
Doran
Nolan
Murphy
McCrath
Hore
Harper
Hogan

Where the remains of the others are buried is now forgotten but some of the bodies were brought across the Boyne and interred in an unmarked common grave near the site of St Finnian's Monastery, where a Protestant church was built in 1808.

In the round-up which followed some men were captured. John Doorly from Lullymore – one of the Kildaremen who stayed with the march – was caught trying to cross the river at Robinson's field.[6] He was marched to Mullingar, where he was hanged. His mother walked the forty miles from her home to beg for his body, so that she might bring it home for burial, but her request was refused.

One young Wexford lad, Jim Doyle, was fifteen or sixteen years of age. After the battle he ran away and lay hidden in a potato field that night, and most of the following day. In the days that followed he was given food and shelter by local families in the area. Eventually he found work with farmers around Kinnegad and Killiwarden and, a few years later, married a local girl. His Doyle descendents are still living in the area.

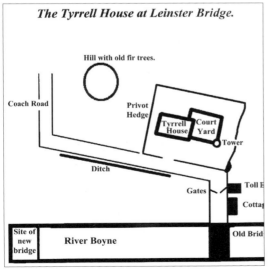

The Tyrrell House at Leinster Bridge.

Hill with old fir trees.

Coach Road

Privot Hedge

Tyrrell House | Court Yard

Tower

Ditch

Gates

Toll

Cotta

Site of new bridge | River Boyne | Old Brid

No plan of the Tyrrell House or surrounding area, as it was in 1798, remains and the above drawing is a reconstruction based on what details are known of the layout. It is not to any scale. The rebels arrived along the coach road and attacked the house. The tower, mentioned in accounts, had a commanding position to fire on the bridge and another contemporary account mentions that some of the Wexfordmen took cover on the hill with the old fir trees. The gates on the approach to the bridge had been closed before the attack commenced.

The Rebels storming "The Turret" at Lieut. Tyrrell's.

George Cruikshank's nineteenth-century representation of the rebel attack on the turret at Leinster Bridge, showing the opening in the ceiling and the difficulty of gaining access to the upper storey. All the indications are that the turret was a round stone building and Cruikshank, who never visited the location, was obviously unaware of this fact when he conceived the drawing, many years afterwards.

The toll house at Leinster Bridge. This early eighteenth-century house served as a toll house until the practice was discontinued. It replaced the toll house which served at the old bridge and which was destroyed during the Battle of Clonard.

Leinster Bridge, Clonard. The present bridge, built in 1831, as seen from the site of the previous bridge, which was in use in 1798.

Clonard. Some of the old walls remaining at the site of the Battle at Clonard.

Another view if the battle site at Leinster Bridge, Clonard. In the background is the hill which may have been used for cover by the Wexfordmen and which was said to have been then covered by fir trees.

Carbury Hill, where the rebel army camped on the night of 11 July 1798.

Newbury Hall, built in 1760, the residence of Lord Harberton, which the rebels occupied when camped at Carbury, and for which a claim for damages caused was subsequently lodged. Lord Harberton was not in residence at the time and, ironically, the insurgents were probably unaware that he was reputedly in sympathy with the United Irishmen and their cause.

The Whitechurch pennant, said to have been captured from the Wexfordmen at the Battle of Clonard on 11 July 1798.

The memorial to Kildareman, John Doorley, at Lullymore.

The house at Teglough where the descendents of Jim Doyle lived until the 1960s. Jim was the young man who escaped after Clonard by hiding for two days in a potato field.

Memorial at Leinster Bridge, Clonard, Co. Kildare:

'Dowd Kiernan Rochford
Sinnott Doyle Redmond
Roach Boland Reilly
Doran Nolan Murphy
McCrath Hore Harpur
Hogan.

Above stand recorded the names of the brave Wexfordmen who fell at Clonard on 11 July 1798, and whose remains lie buried here. Their graves were walled round in 1873 by Mr Garrett Robinson and the Celtic Cross with this memorial slab was erected in 1898 by the priests and people of Ballyna, Kinnegad and Ballybrackey. R.I.P.'

6

Meath:
12 July to 14 July 1798

The rebels arrived at Carbery Hill, in north Kildare, on the evening of 11 July, and made camp there for the night. Some scavenging parties were sent around the area seeking food, arms or any other items useful to their campaign. Amongst the big houses raided was that of Lord Harberton, for which he later petitioned for compensation to the amount of £68 17s 11d, for goods stolen or damaged.[1]

The men from west Wicklow were not, in general, content with the developing situation. Whether Holt's disquiet was spreading through the ranks, whether they had difficulty with the Wexford domination of the leadership, or with the overall plan of campaign, we can not be certain; nor, indeed, do we know how the dissatisfaction was expressed or decided upon. The outcome, however, was a decision, by the majority of the men under Holt, to leave the camp at Carbery and march back directly to Glenmalure. It seems to have been an amicable if, perhaps, regretted parting of the old comrades of many battles, when most of the men of Wicklow set out for home early on the morning of 12 July.

Early on that morning, the main body of the insurgents, now almost exclusively made up of Wexford men, moved up the road towards Johnstown and turned right onto the coach road towards Dublin before turning north again at Nineteenmile House, in the direction of Summerhill.

Forces were now gathering, from all directions, to challenge them and they were being constantly harassed as they progressed. Col. Gough, with a party of the Limerick Regiment and the 7th Dragoon Guards, had left Phillipstown (Daingean) the previous day and was following the rebels at close quarters. At the same time Lt-Col. Gough had left Trim, heading south with part of the Duke of York's Inverness Highlanders, the Trim yeoman cavalry and the Rathcore Rangers. Other forces, from Dublin, Kilcock and Navan, were also moving in the direction of the Wexfordmen.

The rebels halted, at about midday, at Knockderrig Hill[2] a few miles beyond Johnstown and drew up to face Gough – as he described it himself, 'drawn up in a line as really astonished me, with many standards flying and everything prepared to give me battle'.

Gough proved himself a very adept soldier on the occasion, using the terrain to his advantage.[3] He formed a column under the cover of a strong ditch facing the insurgents, who were in open cornfields, where they had been in the act of preparing a meal, and moved up rapidly within range. He surprised his opponents by suddenly opening fire from behind the ditch, which immediately spread confusion and disorder in the camp, with men breaking in many directions and only reforming some distance away to continue their march towards Summerhill.

This was the first instance that the Wexfordmen did not give a good account of themselves in all their weeks of battle and it must be attributed in great measure to the terrible weariness from which they were now suffering, and which was mentioned by many commentators. They had been marching ceaselessly for weeks, constantly fighting battles against fresh, well fed, well trained, and well supplied troops. *Faulkners Journal* described their plight thus:

> These poor wretches were lying in ditches and under hedges, without the least shelter from very inclement weather. They had nothing like uniforms and were only distinguishable from the most miserable of peasantry by carrying pikes and wearing a green cross on their hats and green emblems on their clothes.
>
> And yet they marched on loyally behind their leaders, never suing for terms and, until this day, never turning from a fight. They lost a great deal of their meagre supplies at Knockderrig. Colonel Gough, on taking the hill, reported capturing 40 sheep, 3 bullocks half skinned, a great number of pots boiling, several carloads of flour, groceries, wine and spirits. He also captured a small swivel gun, two casks of powder, a vast quantity of lead and some boxes of swan shot. Also captured was a green silk standard, with a device of a cross and the initials J.H.S., 161 black cattle, 53 horses and 5,000 yards of new linen [bandages].

The insurgents were, nevertheless, a coherent force as they moved on and Gough estimated their number at 4,000, which must have been something of an exaggeration. While there was some degree of fragmentation, as a result of the battle at Knockderrig, nevertheless the main body of the rebel army still held together and marched on towards Longwood, pursued by Gen. Meyrick, and then turned towards Dunboyne, which most reached that night and where they made camp. The difficulties of the insurgents were now beginning to have a major effect on their cohesiveness as a fighting force and, at Dunboyne, for the first time, they no longer seem to have the appearance of a single unit. Stragglers were still coming in along the road from Longwood, probably those too fatigued to keep up with the main group, and some of these were being picked off by the pursuing militia.

Col. Gordon, of the Duke of York's Highlanders, reported that he had pursued the rebels from Longwood to Culmullen and had killed thirty detached parties and stragglers. Many more must have taken to the fields, where they would be found, and killed or captured, in the days that followed.

The omens were not good for the Wexford army as the dawn broke on Friday 13 July. Troops were closing in on them from all quarters. Early that morning Lt Batty had left Balbriggan with the Coolock Cavalry, while Lt Lucas and the Fermanagh Infantry together with the Swords Infantry under Capt. Gordan, also approached from the east. All these forces came together with the Dumfries Fencibles between Ballyboughall and the Naul, together making up a formidable force. At the same time Maj-Gen. Myres, with the Royal Bucks Militia and yeomanry from the garrison of Dublin, had been ordered to pursue the rebels.

Early that morning the Wexfordmen had left the vicinity of Dunboyne and headed for Garristown, once again being constantly harassed as they marched. The Dumfries reported that they had killed ten of the rebel's advance guard near Ballyboughill.

A rather odd occurrence of the day was the capture, by the rebels, of the northbound mail coach that morning at Corduff. The passengers were allowed to make their way back to Dublin but the coach was commandeered. A tantalising scrap of paper has survived on which is written, 'Kane of Wexford, called a general, was at Dunboyne last night with 2000 marching for Fingal. Northern Mail. Murphy in a carriage. Perry, Fitzgerald, Murphy, Keane, Dixon of Castlebridge.

Memorial at Summerhill, Co. Meath.

'Erected to the memory of the Meathmen
and Wexfordmen
who fought and died for freedom
in 1798 and whose remains
lie in the vicinity of
Summerhill, Culmullen and Dunshaughlin.
May God have mercy on their souls.'

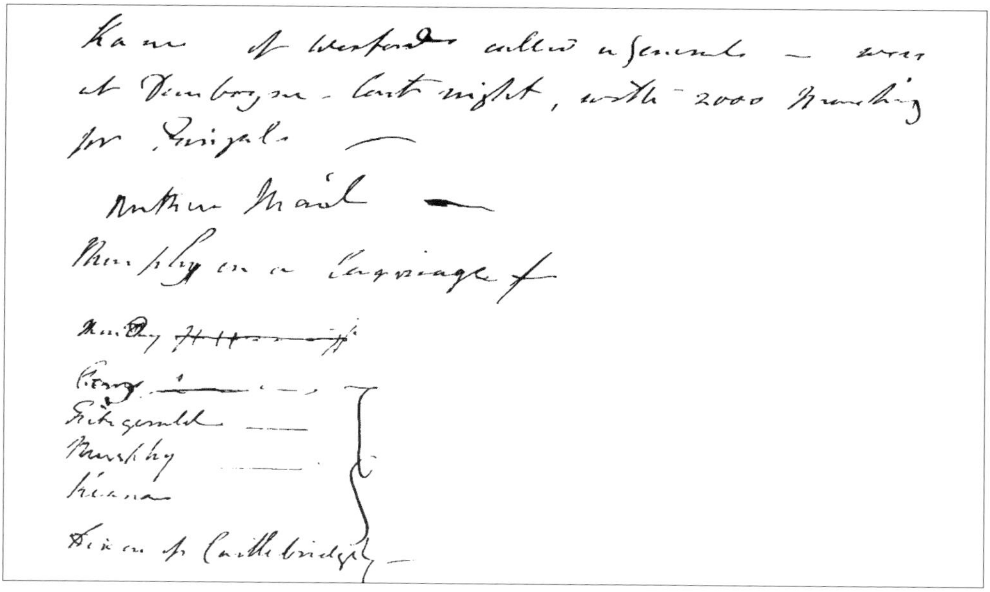

Kane of Wexford called a General — were at Dunboyne last night, with 2000 marching for Fingal —

Northern Mail —

Murphy in a carriage of

Murphy

Perry

Fitzgerald

Murphy

Kearns

Dixon of Castlebridge —

Scrap of paper, possibly part of a hastily scribbled report to Dublin Castle, which states, 'Kane of Wexford called a general – were at Dunboyne last night, with 2,000 marching for Fingal. Northern Mail. Murphy in a carriage – Perry. Fitzgerald. Murphy. Kearns. Dixon of Castlebridge.'

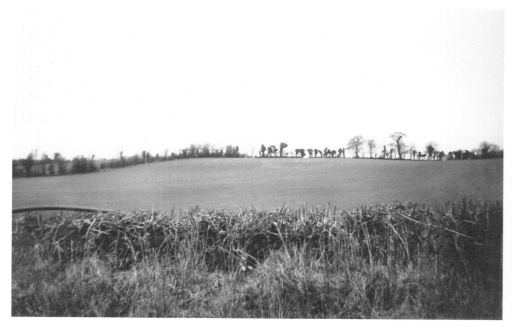

Knockderrig Hill, Rynville.

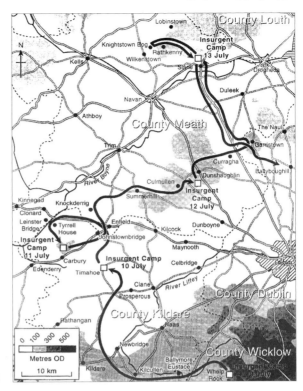

Route taken by the Wexford army.

We can only guess at the significance of this note, which probably constituted part of an intelligence report to Dublin Castle. The mention of Kane is probably a reference to Esmonde Kyan, who was certainly in a leadership position at that time. It is also worth noting that, in a time of poor and uncertain communication, in many quarters it was believed that Fr Murphy was still leading the Wexfordmen, which would help to explain the reference to 'Murphy in a carriage'. Indeed, Gen. Myers himself reported that, 'they were commanded by Murphy, who had been reported to have been killed, Roche, McCann and many others'.

During the morning the rebel army seem to have paused at Garristown Hill, and it may be that they were considering making a stand there, or they may just have stopped to rest, feed and water both men and horses. They were not allowed much time to recuperate for, shortly after they had halted, the troops under Gen. Myers arrived on the scene and the insurgents moved on in some haste, again causing some groups and individuals to lose contact with the main army.

A considerable number of horses fell into the hands of the pursuing soldiers and, according to the *Leinster Journal* of 18 July 1798, 'many were driven into the bogs and ditches, quite overcome with fatigue, perished for the want of strength to disengage themselves.'

The appalling weariness which, by now, affected many of the Wexfordmen can only be imagined. In the weeks since leaving their native county they had marched more than 400 miles pausing, in most cases, only to fight. In an account of the 'croppies' who died at Arodstown, Mary Anne Lynch says, 'a very big crowd came up the field – came from Mr Shannon's field. They were very tired, wounded, hungry and exhausted.'

Despite this the main body, numbering now some 1,500 men, moved along at a brisk pace. Generals Meyrick and Weymes came out of Navan and Drogheda with the express purpose of preventing their move north towards County Cavan but they had, nevertheless, managed to get across the Boyne into County Louth, between Slane and Duleek, late that evening. There they were stopped, however, near Stackallen, by cavalry from the two columns, who had drawn up across the road to Slane.

As an indication that further separation had occurred during the day, a number of scattered skirmishes are reported as having occurred several miles apart at Wilkenstown, Stackallen and Slane, with rebel casualties in all cases. An official report from Weymes states that he arrived at Duleek at ten o'clock that night and that the main rebel group were strongly posted on a hill three miles to his right (across the Boyne). He may have been in error here, as the main body would seem to have moved some hours earlier a few miles further west to Slane, where they encamped, possibly leaving part of their force nearer to Duleek.

Shortly after dawn, on the morning of 14 July 1798, the Wexford army moved away from the area of Slane. About the same time a small party of about 100 struck out eastward towards Ardee, but were stopped from progressing very far along the road and were dispersed. This was hardly a tactic on the part of the insurgents, but would rather appear to confirm that groups were failing to keep up with the main army and losing touch under the terrible pressure now being applied on them from all sides. The main body moved north-eastwards towards Rathkenny,[6] their only plan to try and shake off their pursuers and make their way north, where they might find some support and relief. At this stage they would have numbered little over 1,000 men, over 400 of whom were mounted. The high proportion of horsemen remaining amongst the group once again highlights the very great difficulty those on foot must have found in keeping up with the constant brisk pace of the march. By now their supplies too must have been well nigh exhausted, with powder and shot being particularly scarce.

Shortly after the Wexfordmen left Slane, Gen. Weymes, with a Mr Trotter of Duleek acting as a guide, arrived there, as did Gen. Dundas, coming from the opposite direction. They consulted at Lord Boyne's residence after being told that the rebels had left and headed north. Gen. Meyrick ordered Lt-Col. Orde, with the Durham Cavalry, to overtake them and keep them in check until the main force could come up.

The first contact between the opposing forces occurred about half past nine at a bridge along the route, when the cavalry closed up with the rebel rearguard in an attempt to impede their progress. The precise location of this 'old dilapidated bridge' is no longer clear but it would seem, almost certainly, to have been over one of the small streams along the old road from Rathkenny to Clynch, and to the west of Chamberstown Hill.

The Wexfordmen were forced to turn and make a charge on the Durhams and they fell back, allowing the rebels to cross. A group of pikemen, under the command of a Wexford townman named Bryan, was then left to hold the narrow bridge and, after a short and bloody skirmish, casualties were suffered on both sides. Further reinforcements of cavalry had been ordered forward and the came up on the insurgents at Knightstown Bog, near to Wilkenstown and between Nobber and Navan, at a place just off the Navan to Kingscourt road. It was about eleven o'clock in the morning.

The insurgents were on a slight rise of ground, behind a defile and between two bogs. They were drawn up in an orderly and disciplined line. Anthony Perry, who had seen action in the American War of Independence, was in command and was not disposed to enter a contest if it could be avoided. With horses and men at near exhaustion and short of powder and shot he was, beyond any doubt, fully aware of the desperate weakness of his position. It is a tribute to the Wexfordmen's courage and loyalty that, even now, when almost beyond hope, they faced their enemies in an orderly line of battle.[7] Not alone that, with a loud rebel yell, they made a spirited charge, which forced the Dumfries to draw back. Meyrick was certainly impressed and, by his own admission, was compelled to fall back and await the arrival of the arrival of the artillery. This arrived shortly afterwards with the Northumberland Highlanders and it was this that put the issue beyond doubt.

The insurgent pikes were no answer to canister and grapeshot, which inflicted severe casualties on the rebel line. The first fusillade killed thirty of the insurgents and wounded many more. Further fire continued to inflict casualties on those who could do nothing but seek shelter behind the dead horses. We have no way of knowing what was happening in the rebel camp or how the decision was made but, about midday, a general dispersal of the rebel army occurred. This may have been spontaneous, and brought on by the ferocity of the attack, or it may have resulted from a decision by the leaders that the situation had become hopeless and that the best chance of survival lay in separating into individuals and groups. It is remembered that somebody shouted the order, 'Whelan lead for the road. Men follow him' and Timothy Whelan, from Askasillagh, Blackwater, County Wexford turned and made for the road leading towards Ardee.

Those on foot headed into the fields all round the area and many were quickly cut down by the cavalry as they sought to make their escape, while others managed to get beyond the immediate area of the battle, to be hunted in the days and weeks to follow. Everything was left behind and one government report states, 'we took a great quantity of pikes, pistols, swords, muskets and two standards'.[8] It is notable, however, that no powder or shot is mentioned as having been captured. Meyrick also pointedly reports that he took 'one prisoner'.

One large group, however, consisting of about 350 men on horseback, did manage to avoid contact with the enemy and set off to the east at a brisk pace towards Ardee, before turning south to cross the Boyne again at Slane. They were hotly pursued by cavalry lead by Col. Gordon. It was too much for many and one of the pursuers, Capt. Barry, reported that he found on the road several pikes and took ten tired horses.

By evening the riders had reached Garristown, where they had halted on the previous day, and headed down the hill towards Oldtown and Ballyboughill. They could go no further. At a sharp bend, less than a mile from Ballyboughill, with horses and men totally exhausted, they left the road and formed up in a field about 200 yards away.

Many were, by now, totally unarmed as was admitted by Lt Barry of the Coolock Cavalry. Of those who had guns all but a few were without powder or shot. On the approach of the cavalry they formed up and, in one last act of desperate defiance, fired their last few shots, killing only one horse.

It fell to Esmond Kyan to be the last commander of the army of the Wexford Republic, which had begun its campaign at the Harrow seven weeks earlier. Kyan was a courageous and honourable man who, though he had only the use of one hand, had fought gallantly from the start and had been in command of the insurgent artillery at the Battle of Arklow. He said goodbye and ordered his men to disperse so that they might have a chance to escape. Then the rebels quickly broke in all directions into the cornfields of north county Dublin, around Ballyboughill and the Naul, many of them to be cruelly cut down by their pursuers. Batty boasted that more than 150 rebels had been killed.

This then was the final hour of the army of Wexfordmen, who had left Carraigrue Hill a couple of weeks before and crossed over the Wicklow border, like a lost army never to return. Nothing was left but, across the plains of Meath from Clonard in the south, to Nobber on the borders of Cavan, the fugitives, the prisoners, the wounded and the dead.

On the road near Clynch, Co. Meath, the likely location of the 'Battle of the Bridge'.

Culmullen Cross showing the road the Insurgents took.

The Memorial at Grange, Co. Meath:

'This monument was erected in 1952
In proud memory of the insurgents
Who made their last stand
In Knightstown bog
On 14th of July 1798 the remains of whom
Lie in the fields and roadsides of this district.
May God have mercy on their souls.'

Garristown Hill, where the rebels paused briefly on Friday, 13 July 1798.

The bleak site of the rebel stand at Knightstown bog.

The unveiling of the memorial at Slane in 1951 by Government Minister, Dr James Ryan. The legend reads, 'This monument was erected to the memory of the Wexford column who, in July 1798, fought and died for the freedom of Ireland in the Slane area and whose remains are buried in the surrounding districts. Also in memory of the Meathmen who, in 1798, rose and died that Ireland might be free.' Erected by Slane 1798 committee August 1951.

The Boyne Bridge at Slane which some of the Wexford army crossed on the evening of 13 July 1798.

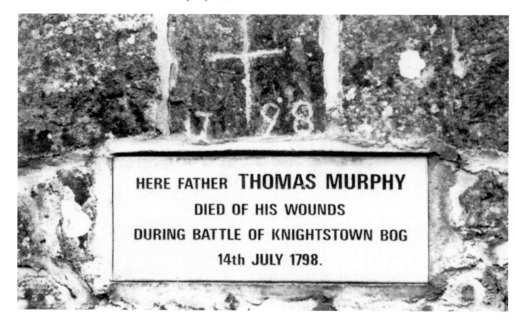

HERE FATHER **THOMAS MURPHY**
DIED OF HIS WOUNDS
DURING BATTLE OF KNIGHTSTOWN BOG
14th JULY 1798.

Drakestown Bridge. One of the most mysterious and intriguing events of the rebellion took place on this little bridge on the Sunday afternoon of 14 July 1798, with the killing there of one of the rebels by local yeomany members, 'Squire' Thomas Corbally, who was a coachman, Jackson, Naulty and Smith. Strong local tradition and contemporary sources claim that the rebel who was killed was, 'Father Murphy who was a chaplain to the insurgents'. It has been difficult to identify a third priest named Murphy associated with the rebels but the evidence that he was Fr Thomas Murphy, brother of Fr Michael Murphy, killed at Arklow, is difficult to ignore. The details of the killing are recorded by many different sources, one saying, 'Corbally and Jackson gave Father Tom his death. The priest was on the bridge when the final blow came and he laid his head down on the wall and died.' The cross and date 1798 have been inscribed on one of the stones longer than anyone remembers and, in 1998 a stone was unveiled beneath this bearing the legend 'Here Father Thomas Murphy died of his wounds during the Battle of Knightstown Bog 14th July 1798'.

Perry and Kearns:
14 July to 21 July 1798

It is perhaps appropriate to follow the fate of two of the principal leaders, Col Anthony Perry and Fr Mogue Kearns, at this point. Not a great amount of detail is on record with regard to their leadership from the time they left Carraigrue until they arrived at Clonard, after which there is a good deal of conflict in the accounts of their movements and activities.

The principal problem is one of chronology, to which the dates of their capture and execution are central. There are a number of differing accounts giving the date of the taking of the leaders, ranging from 12 July to 18 July, many of them clearly impossible in the light of well documented evidence. The most persistent error is that which records their death as being on 12 July, and which is, incidentally, repeated on both the Kearns memorial at Kiltealy and that near the site of his birthplace. For this date to have been correct the overwhelming evidence of their later participation would have to be ignored.

There is no doubt, for instance, that Perry moved on into Meath and was in command at Knightstown on 14 July. Luke Cullen records that:

The battles that he fought in I received in an account from my father, who was never parted from Perry until the day that he and Fr Kearns parted with the people and went to the King's county. His battles were Arklow, Vinegar Hill, Hacketstown, Ballyellis, Ballyraheen, Clonard and Knightstown Bog beside several skirmishes in going and returning from Meath.

There can be little doubt that the date of the capture of the leaders was 18 July and their execution date was 21 July, being the only dates which fit with all the accepted incidents with which they are clearly associated.

Col. Anthony Perry, from Inch in the north of County Wexford, was a Protestant landowner, who was married to a Catholic. The son of a Dublin cardmaker, he saw action as an officer in the British army during the American War of Independence and, on his return, married a Catholic, Eliza Ford, from Ballyfad, near to his home in Perrymount.

He was an important member and organiser of the Society of United Irishmen, while still a member in the local Yeomanry, but publicly quit the yeomanry when he could no longer stand their excesses. He was arrested on the outbreak of the insurrection and cruelly tortured in Gorey by the brutal 'Tom the Devil', but was released when Gorey fell to the rebels, and led a group of the released prisoners to Carraigrue. From then on he was one of the principal leaders, notable for the military experience which he brought to the rebel army.

Fr Kearns, on the other hand, was more a man of the people, whose leadership position came from a background representative of the rank and file of the insurgent army. He was a farmer's son from Kiltealy, beneath the Blackstairs Mountains, and was first cousin to another of the insurgent leaders, John Kelly of Kilanne. He was a very big man, some said 6ft 6ins tall, and, in his youth, had achieved fame as a hurler.

He went to Paris to study for the priesthood and was there during the Revolution, which must have had a big influence on his political thinking.

While he may have proved himself a man of the people, he was not, seemingly, held in the same high regard by his bishop, Dr Caulfield of Ferns. Dr Caulfield wrote, in a letter to Dr Troy, Archbishop of Dublin, after the end of the outbreak, 'Rev. Mogue Kearns of the Duffry had been employed by Dr Delaney (Kildare and Leighlin) for some time, but lately dismissed. He was notorious for drinking and fighting; and joined the rebels among whom he made a gigantic figure, and was hanged at Edenderry.'

The notable point here is not the disenchantment which his Lordship expresses with Fr Kearns, but the fact that he was employed in the dioceses Kildare and Leighlin rather than Ferns. He was, in fact, for some years, a curate in Ballyna, in north Kildare, near the conjunction of counties Meath, Westmeath and Kildare, and just a few miles from Clonard, where he was involved in the fighting. While serving there he had, undoubtedly, made friends and contacts and had become conversant with the surrounding country; and he had actually, on more than one occasion, visited Mrs Tyrrell, wife of the High Sheriff, and her family at their house at Kilriney. While stationed in Ballyna he was politically active and his parish priest, Fr Michael Corcoran – later to become Bishop of Kildare and Leighlin – opposed his views strenuously which was, in all probability, the principal reason for his transfer to Enniscorthy in his native County Wexford.

After the Battle of Knightstown, on the morning of Saturday 14 July 1798, with the effective disbandment of the rebel army, Kearns and Perry stayed together and headed south-west towards County Westmeath. The next certain location in which we find them is, hiding out, more than fifty miles away, in the area of Ballynagore, about ten miles south of Mullingar. They might have reached here late on the night of 14 July but, allowing for the fact that they would have had to avoid enemy patrols, and taken back roads around towns like Navan, Kells and Mullingar and, of course, the fact that fifty miles in one day is on the extreme range of even a very sound and rested horse, it is much more likely that they reached Ballynagore some time on 15 July.

It is not known where they were given shelter, but it is reasonable to assume that it was with a supporter of their cause or, perhaps, a personal friend of Kearns. Their hiding place became known and there is a persistent tradition that they were, in fact, captured in Ballynagore, but, with help, managed to make their escape. An account given by Liam Moran, speaking of Kearns, tells us that, 'the men of Ballynagore who captured him were men named Lows and Robinson', and goes on to describe how they were bound and left on their horses, while the yeomen went to eat. Two young sisters, looking out from an upstairs window, were persuaded to come down and release them.

For whatever reason, the pair of leaders certainly left Ballynagore in haste and, pursued by Robinson, headed to Clonbullogue, where they stayed, on the night of 17 July, with the Lynam family at Ballynowlart North. There are no Lynams in the parish of Clonbullogue today, but school records of 1876 show the Lynams were still there at that time and, descendents, through the female line, are still living in the townland. Tradition tells us that Fr Kearns said mass in the Lynam house, before leaving, early on the morning of 18 July.

The hunt was now on in earnest and the authorities were well aware that the two Wexfordmen were in the vicinity. Capt. Ridgeway, of the Edenderry yeomanry, and Robinson, together with about fifteen men, arrived in Clonbullogue on the morning of Wednesday, 18 July, enquiring if Perry and Kearns had passed through the village. At the forge they asked the smith – a Protestant named Flynn – and his brother if they had seen the fugitives. Both denied that they had seen them, though they had, just minutes earlier, been at the forge seeking to have one of their horses shod. The search party then headed out the Rathangan road but had only gone a short distance when a man, standing in a doorway, shouted that the fugitives had gone the Bracknagh road.[1] Ridgeway immediately turned his horse and he and his group galloped back the road towards Bracknagh.

Kearns and Perry had become separated from their horses at this stage. It has been suggested that the horses were in Flynn's forge being shod, when the search party arrived looking for the rebel leaders, and that they made a hasty escape on foot. On the other hand they may have deliberately chosen to travel on foot, perhaps believing that it would allow them to hide more easily in the woods and bogs of the area. They were making their way along the road towards Bracknagh, when they were overtaken by Ridgeway, Robinson and party, and placed under arrest.

The place where they were taken is only a short distance out of Clonbullogue at a spot called the 'Wheel-about', in the townland of Derrymore. There is a little bridge there, thirty paces beyond which, it is said, is the exact spot where the leaders were apprehended. The two were bound, and marched the six miles back to Edenderry, where they were closely questioned by Ridgeway, who presided at the subsequent trial. Needless to say they were both sentenced to death.

On Saturday morning 21 July, they were brought up the hill to Blundell Wood, overlooking the town. A large crowd had gathered to witness the execution and the rope was fixed to the branch of a stout oak tree in a small wood. Perry was first to hang and submitted to his fate with a quiet fortitude. When the time came to hang Kearns, he smiled as the rope was placed around his neck, but, when dropped, the rope failed to run through the loop and he was not fully dead when taken down.[2] The members of the local Yeomanry then cut off his head with an axe, and further mutilated his body.

There are two versions of what then happened to the remains, one based on local tradition and one on more reliable evidence. The bodies of both men are interred at Monasteroris graveyard, about a mile outside the town. Some doubt remains, however, about the head of Fr Kearns. The intention was that his head should be spiked for all to see as they passed, but a local woman, Catherine O'Connell, it is said, retrieved the head and carried it, in her apron, to Monasteroris, where it was buried in the O'Connell plot.

About the end of the 1960s, however, Fr Joseph Hurley S.J., a well-known Gaelic scholar and editor of *Timthire An Chroidhe Naomhtha*, discovered what was claimed to be the head of Mogue Kearns in Cambridge University, and, subsequently, buried it at Moneteroris with his body. Ridgeway had a son, who was Protestant rector in Rathangan and Clonbullogue, whose own son was to become Sir William Ridgeway, a celebrated Brehon scholar and antiquarian in Cambridge. The skull of the patriot was not, apparently, rescued by Mrs O'Connell, but was kept by the yeoman captain, who passed it down through his descendents until it found its way to Cambridge.

The axe used to sever the head was kept in a chest in Edenderry Orange lodge and Kearns' horse, which was recovered from wheresoever it had been abandoned, was kept by Ridgeway, who named it 'Kearns'. Of Kearns, Myles Byrne was to say, 'Had he been bred to the military profession in a country like France, where courage and merit were sure of being recompensed, he would have been a Kleber, and soon have been raised to the first rank in any army he made part of.'

A fine celtic cross now marks the graves of Perry and Kearns in Monasteroris cemetary and each has a street named in his honour in Edenderry town.

Ballinagore, Co. Westmeath, where Perry and Kearns were given shelter.

Clonbullogue. The road to the left is the Rathangan road, being taken by Robinson and the pursuing party when they were told that Perry and Kearns had gone to the right towards Bracknagh. The forge owned by the Flynn brothers was sited near the buildings towards the right of the photograph.

Local man, Denis Kelly, photographed in 1996, pointing to the spot at Wheel-about, Clonbullogue, Co. Offaly, where Fr Mogue Kearns and Anthony Perry were captured.

The site of the execution of Perry and Kearns at Blundell Wood, Edenderry, Co. Offaly on 21 July 1798.

'Erected to the memory of
Rev. Moses Kearns C.C.
And Colonel Anthony Perry
who were executed for their love
of country at Edenderry
In the memorable year of 1798
R.I.P.
God Save Ireland.'

8

Fugitives

The collapse of the insurgent army, on 14 July, left about 1,500 Wexfordmen stranded as fugitives in County Meath, spreading out, along their line of march, over a distance of nearly fifty miles. The were gathered in numbers ranging from groups of fifty or more down to single individuals, seeking whatever shelter they could find in the woods, ditches and wheat fields throughout the area. Given the nature of society at the time, many of them might, never before, have been outside the borders of their native county and now, 150 miles from their homes, and no longer under any clear leadership, they must have been at a great loss to know where to turn. They were in strange surroundings with no familiar landmarks and without the comforting sight of Mount Leinster on the skyline to show them in what direction their beloved Wexford lay.

Most were hungry and tired and more than a few were ill or wounded. Badly armed or, indeed, without arms of any kind, they were at the mercy of the troops and yeomanry hunting them with vigour. They were shown ery little mercy for, while some prisoners were taken as we shall see, the killing of rebels where and when discovered was the order of the day. They were given no respite for the hunt began immediately following the dispersal at Knightstown, where many had sought shelter in the surrounding bogs. A contemporary account of the time tells the story:

> The rebels got into the bogs and the cavalry advanced and killed all they met with and surrounded the bog to the right. On the opposite side, the Highlanders got into the bog and killed all that were in it. Those who got out on the opposite side were met with the cavalry. From the manner in which they dispersed I cannot give an exact account of the killed.[1]

In a few cases a bare token of restraint seems to have been shown by some of the Highlanders. An official report, dated 15 July 1798, reads:

> I have the honour also to inform you that a detachment of my Reg. came up yesterday with a party of the rebels consisting of sixteen with as many horses – the rebels fired on my detachment without effect, who attacked them and killed fifteen and brought one prisoner in, a very young boy who was a servant of Capt. Knox Grogan who was killed in Wicklow – the boy is most intelligent and I expect to have the honour of sending some useful information to your Lordship tomorrow.[2]

With the passing of time the chances of survival improved, though not significantly, but, in the following days, many managed to travel some little distance from the centre of activity. In a good many cases they were helped, at very great risk to themselves, by local people.

Unlike some parts through which the Wexfordmen had fought, the people of Meath were, by and large, sympathetic to the rebels and their cause. The United Irish movement has been strong in County Meath. In 1797, the Provincial Report had given their strength as 7,922. By February 1798, captured documents showed the strength in the county as 14,000 and a return, subsequently found in the house of Edward Rattigan in Dublin, showed that they had nearly 500 guns and 17 pounds of powder, 17 small cannon and 940 cannon balls. They rose at the end of May but, while they had some initial success, they were overcome, with the loss of many killed and captured.

Charles Teeling puts the lack of success in Meath squarely on the lack of efficient officers, with tactical skill and overall strategic comprehension. Meath was also, in some ways, similar to Wexford in its type of farming and, to a lesser extent, cultural background. So, while only a handful of Meathmen actively fought with the Wexfordmen, the local people, in the main, supported their cause and were disposed to help them where they could.

Even in defeat the spectre of the rebels was still causing panic in many quarters. Two days after the Battle of Knightstown an express message came from a Col. Cole with the extraordinary claim that 13,000 rebels had collected on an island in the great bog which divides Meath from Westmeath, and the chief constable of Navan reported, at the same time, that, 'several of the rebels have been killed this day and some taken prisoner' but added, 'I had a very narrow escape of being taken yesterday by about fifty of the rebels'. And, despite their desperate situation, some were, indeed, making every effort to continue the fight to the last. As late as 24 July, Col. Gordon reported to Lord Castlerea:

> Hearing of a party of rebels who were infesting country between Summerhill and Kilcock, I sent out a party last night at 12 o'clock from this, of Light Dragoons and an infantry soldier mounted behind each of them, which they did and killed several of the rebels who fired on them without effect. The extreme badness of the night and neighbouring woods favoured the escape of the few who were not killed.

An account of the sad end of some of the men from Wexford is recorded in a footnote in the *Diocese of Meath* by Cogan, regarding the experience of Revd Patrick Langan PP:

> He was master of the Deanery of Rathoath. In the year 1798, three Wexford men, who had remained behind from the main body, were overtaken near Rathoath by the savage yeomanry, and were ordered to be instantly hanged. The poor fellows begged and supplicated for a priest and Lord Fingal, being one of the officers in Command, dispatched a messenger for Fr. Langan. The soldiers, who were with difficulty restrained from executing them without allowing them the benefit of the sacraments in the wood near Rathoath, and they were launched into eternity.

Local tradition carried many accounts of the hunting and capture of the rebels, such as the murder of twenty-one insurgents caught hiding in Lawless's barn near Gaulstown. They were surrounded in the building and some were shot as they tried to escape, while those captured were immediately hanged nearby.

Another gives an account of a group, who were being hidden, at Morgan's of The Deans, in a wicker loft in the barn. Morgan informed Capt. Dillon of Mannastown, a captain in the Yeomanry, who came with a troop and killed them as they slept.

With the passing of time, and the country coming back under the clear control of the authorities, the pressure seems to have reduced somewhat on those managing to remain at large. The bloodlust of the yeomanry may have been sated to a degree or, perhaps, many of them tired of the chase. Some of the Wexford men began to find ways of survival. There are stories of them working with local farmers throughout many parts of Meath from Carolanstown to Dunleer.

There is one account, for instance, from John Kiely (born 1867) of a man named Coffey, a schoolmaster from County Wexford, who survived and later managed to build a house, with the help of local people, at Greenhills, Newtown, Ardee. He eventually married and had one son and one daughter, all of whom are buried locally in Syddan cemetery.

Another account, from the same John Kiely, tells of a man named McEvoy, who also came with the rebel army, and who married and lived, with his family, at Rathban Mor. John Kiely, himself, knew some of his children, one of whom was named Owen McEvoy.[3]

Some found other means of survival, as will be clearly shown by a letter written by a Henry Baker in Balbriggan on 30 October, nearly four months after the Battle of Knightstown Bog, and addressed to Edward Cooke at Dublin Castle:

> Sir, I was credibly informed that a Wexford man, who had been wounded in the leg at Ballybohill the 14th July last remained in the county, that he headed a party of robbers and was endeavouring to disturb this neighbourhood. I therefore took a party out some nights since and apprehended him in a house near the Bog of the Ring. From information I have received I believe he was one of the rebels we engaged at Ballybohill on 14th July.

He calls himself Edwd O'Neill, Coogan or Hogan. Captain Bellock of Dumf', who commands here, has ordered a party to escort this man to the Provost tomorrow.

Almost certainly most of the fugitives would have tried to make their way home to their native Wexford but many, alas, found the task beyond them. Miles Byrnes records in his memoirs, 'About this time I received a letter from Nick Murphy of Monaseed, who escaped from the Boyne and got into Dublin, where he was hiding as well as hundreds of our comrades. Their escape, as well as his, seemed miraculous.' But, later on, Byrne sadly records, 'Many of the brave county of Wexford men, who escaped from the disasters of the Boyne, took refuge in Booterstown lane and were living in wretched little cabins in the back alleys, with their female relations, mothers, sisters, wives etc., all having abandoned their homes.'

Some insurgents did, eventually, manage to get back to their homes in Wexford but who they were, or how many, we shall never know. In his notes on 'The Battle of Oulart Hill', Brian Cleary records the names of five who did: Ryan, Dempsey, Mythen, Kinsella and Joe Doyle. As for the remainder some, who had not been killed or captured, were still in Meath long afterwards and some, indeed, seem to have managed to redeem themselves in the eyes of the authorities. A letter of 24 August 1799, perhaps demonstrates that a somewhat more pragmatic policy was being adopted by the government a year after the rebellion: 'Delivered to His Excellency by Lord Fingall – Mr. Marsden is requested to give these persons such assurances of protection as may be consistant and proper.'[4]

The names of the rebels recommended for protection by Lord Fingall were:

William Carton, Ballyclough, farmer
Nicholas Murphy, Monaseed, farmer and shopkeeper
James D'Arcy, Monclane, farmer
Denis Redmond, Kilcavan, house carpenter
Jn' Redmond Jun' Kilcavan

9

Prisoners

Though many of the men who marched into Meath were killed, often in cold blood, as fugitives, a good number were, nevertheless, taken prisoner, mainly after the collapse of the insurgent army on 14 July. The most significant figure, perhaps, apart from Perry and Kearns,[1] to fall into the hands of the authorities, was the very popular leader Edward Fitzgerald of Newpark. There is little clarity about the circumstances of his surrender except for the fact that he gave himself up to Gen. Dundas and his troops in north Kildare, together with the Kildare rebels under Aylmer, on 21 July. The Kildaremen had been seeking terms for surrender and one account of the events asserts that Fitzgerald himself, with William Aylmer of Rathcoffey, signed a treaty at Rathcoffey under which arms were to be handed in at Ballygoran Hill near Maynooth. This treaty allowed a full pardon for the rank and file of the Kildare rebels, while their leaders were to be exiled.

Fitzgerald did not favour the strategy of moving into Meath and he was probably one of those who argued against leaving the protection of the Wicklow mountains. He separated from the main army on or before the 12 July. Apart from the small scrap of paper which suggests that he was in Dunboyne on the 12 July, there is no account of his movements at all. It is virtually certain that he did not march on to Clonard with the others on 11 July, but, perhaps thinking it folly, remained with Aylmer until their surrender at Maynooth. The leaders, including Fitzgerald, were taken in five carriages to Dublin Castle and became the first principals of the rebellion to escape execution or murder.

Throughout Meath and north County Dublin prisoners were being taken singly and in small groups over a period of months, following the dispersal of the Wexford army. The first report of captives relates to the day after the battle at Knightstown, when Gen. Alex Campbell reported that five people had been taken as prisoners by the yeomanry near Ardee and were confined at Dundalk. He stated that they belonged to the 'Body of Rebels' and had been found hiding in the cornfields the day after their companions had been dispersed at Knightstown.[2] This particular group of prisoners were amongst the fortunate few treated with some humanity, probably by virtue of the fact that their trial seems to have been postponed for more than three months. Part of a letter from Charles Fitzroy, dated 22 October 1798, reads as follows:

> There are five other men that never had been tried. They are Wicklowmen and were taken near Ardee, owing themselves to have been with the rebels, but as they say, in the act of coming to Ardee for a protection. I thought if I had ordered them to be tried so long after the fact by English Militia Officers they would have got off, therefore I told them if they preferred being kept prisoners till our county was quiet to standing the chance of a Court Martial, I would then consider their confinement as a sufficient punishment and release them. This they jumped at and unless I receive directions to the contrary, I shall allow them sixpence a day and release them when I think there will be no danger of adding fuel to the fire by turning them into their own county.[3]

Information was coming in from many quarters telling of the whereabouts of the insurgents and parties were being dispatched to kill or capture them. A gentleman named Marcus Somerville reported, on 22 August, that he had heard that six Wexford rebels, armed with as many blunderbusses, were being employed by a farmer named Garrett at the Lough of the Bay.[4] He went on to say that they took their arms to bed with them at night and, every morning, brought them with them to the fields under their greatcoats. He wondered would it be better to attack them when they were sleeping in the farmer's barn or to surround them in the fields while they were reaping with their comrades. What eventually happened to this group of Wexfordmen we are not told.

The first General Court Martial following the fighting in Meath was assembled at Slane, only four days after Knightstown, on 18 July 1798, by the order of Gen. Meyrick.[5] The members were: Capt. Lambert (President), Capt. Gethin, Lt Blakeny, Lt Sillery and Lt Colello. Charges were against, 'sundry persons, of which the late Thomas Dogherty was one' in the case of the King against: Anthony Cavanagh. Thomas Farrell. Peter Kirwan. James Tongue. Matthew Byrne. Dan Hanlon. Bryan Byrne. Charles Byrne. Thomas Dogerty. Patrick Byrne. Luke Reilly. Mich Byrne. John Flynn. Mich O'Neill. Philip Carney. Thomas Magrane.

They were charged with waging war against, 'our Soverign Lord the King and his Liege Subjects, with intent to overturn our happy Constitution, and that you with several others were in arms and did oppose His Majesty's Forces.'

All the prisoners pleaded not guilty but the court brought in a verdict of guilty and sentenced Thomas Dogherty to death. The eventual fate of all those taken into custody – death, transportation or imprisonment – is another day's work, but we have one record of the details of some of those captured after the excursion into Meath. This is part of the list of prisoners on board the hired tender *Columbine*[6] dated 25 September 1798, and giving a number of details of number, name, age, height, description, where taken up and by whom and their crime. It makes interesting reading:

1. Hugh Lacey. 22. 5–3. Brown Hair. A little deaf. Kingscourt Co. Cavan. Lower Kells Cavalry. With the rebels.
2. Matthew Byrne. 29. 5–6. Black Hair. Co. Meath. Yeoman Cavalry. Being with the rebels.
3. John Byrne. 21. 5–10. Black Hair, Kull Mullen (*Culmullen*), Co. Meath. Lord Fingal's Cavalry. Being with the rebels.
4. James Lacy. 25. 5–5. Brown Hair. Kull Mullen (*Culmullen*), Co. Meath. Lord Fingal's Cavalry. Being with the rebels.
5. Laurence Murray. 18. 5–5. Brown Hair. Rofoy (*Rathfeigh*), Co. Meath. Buckingham Militia. Being with the rebels.
6. Bryan Byrne. 57. 5–6. Near Slayn (*Slane*), Co. Meath. Squire Morris. Being with the rebels.
7. Daniel Hanlen. 29. 5–4. Black Hair. Near Slayn (*Slane*), Co. Meath. Yeoman cavalry. Being with the rebels.
8. John Callaghan. 33. 5–3. Brown Hair. Gave himself up to the Carlow Militia in Navan. Being out in the night.
9. Murthe Casey. 46. 5–2. Black Hair. Near Navan, Co. Meath. Nobber Cavalry. Being with the rebels.
10. Patrick Murray. 44. 5–6. Black Hair. Gave himself up in Navan to the Navan Cavalry. Being with the rebels.
11. Darby Byrne. 18. 5–8. Brown Hair. Kull Mullen (*Culmullen*), Co. Meath. Lord Fingal's Cavalry. Being with the rebels.
12. Patrick Shanon. 24. 5–2. Black Hair. Gave himself up in Navan to a yeoman. Being with the rebels.
13. Patrick McDaniel. 33. 5–3. Very bad with a rupture. Gave himself up near Dundhaughlin to Lord Fingal's Cavalry. With the rebels.
14. Hugh Madden. 25. 5–4. Brown Hair. Tankerstown. (*Tankardstown*). Yeoman Cavalry. With the rebels.
15. Daniel Fogharty. 55. 5–2. Black Hair. Navan, Co. Meath. Navan Cavalry. With the rebels.
16. Joseph Murphy. 21. 5–5. Black Hair. County Meath. Lord Fingal's Cavalry. With the rebels.
17. Luke Reilly. 24. 5–8. Black Hair. Co. Meath. Lord Fingal's Cavalry. On suspicion.
18. Thomas Dillon. 22. 5–6. Red Hair. Co. Meath. Lord Fingal's Cavalry. On suspicion.
19. Thomas Maileia. 26. 5–7. Dark Hair. Dunshaughlin. Police. On suspicion.
20. John Early. 23. 5–8. Dark Hair. Co. Meath. A Mr. Wolfe. On suspicion.
21. William Lord. 35. 5–4. Black Hair. Shot through the cheek. Co. Meath. He believes police. On suspicion.
22. Matthew Hanlen. 23. 5–6. Red Hair. Co. Meath. Lord Fingal. On suspicion.
23. John Hopkins. 22. 5–8. Dark Hair. Navan, Co. Meath. Yeoman Cavalry. On suspicion.
24. Daniel Byrne. 21. 5–9. Brown Hair. Navan, Co. Meath. Drumcondra Infantry Corps. On suspicion.
25. Patrick Byrne. 56. 5–9. Wears a wig. Navan, Co. Meath. Yeoman Cavalry. On suspicion.

26. Peter Monahan. 16. 5–5. Brown Hair. Navan, Co. Meath. Lord Fingal's Cavalry. On suspicion.
27. Thomas Logan. 15. 5–0. Dark Hair. Navan Co. Meath. Lower Kells Cavalry. On suspicion.

There follows a tantalising gap in the records, leaving us to wonder who the next sixty-one rebels in captivity were, before the final entry:

89. Francis Duffy. 30. 5–10. Brown Hair. Castlejordan, Co. Meath. Kinnegad Yeomanry. Swore an oath of secrecy.

10

Wounded

After the fighting in Meath a number of rebels were treated in hospital by Dr Maurice Neligan of Navan. The dates of their treatment range from 12 July to 22 August indicating, perhaps, that they were listed as they were captured or surrendered themselves for treatment. A document, signed by Brig.-Gen. Merrick gives us some interesting details:

Sir,

I take the liberty of enclosing the certificate of my attendance on the sick and wounded rebel prisoners confined in Navan signed by General Merrick, commanding in this district and would have made this application long since but was informed it would also be necessary for Captain Preston to sign it being also quartered in the town at the time, which I could not possibly get done as Captain Preston went to England immediately on the countrys being quieted and did not return until the meeting of Parliament. If you will pleased to run your eye over the list you will find a great many ill of fever, which they brought with them here and it was of the most malignant kind and were it not for the very good care I took of them, with exceeding great hazard to myself, I have every reason to believe it would have spread through the country, for notwithstanding every possible attention to air and cleanliness, the servants of both milk woman and baker who attended them took it and were with difficulty saved.

The attendance on the prisoners exceeded thirty eight days whose whole number amounted to-------.

I have also enclosed you a certificate of my attention to the troops regulars as well as Yeomanry, signed by Lord Fingall and Captain Preston, men who have had frequent opportunities of witnessing it for which you will please to observe.

I claim no recompense and mention it only to show you I am not undeserving of the attention of Government who I am confident will appreciate my services as they deserve and

I am Sir
Your most Obed and Humble Servant,
Maurice Neligan. 18th of March 1800.

The attached certificate, signed by Brig.-Gen. Merrick, gives the list of the men treated, their wounds or illness and the results of the treatment by Dr Neligan. It is worth noting that the doctor claims to have cured all those he treated, with problems ranging from rheumatism to fractures of the skull:

Dr Neligan of Navan attended the wounded at Tara and in the county Meath.
We certify that Dr Neligan of Navan in the County of Meath has frequently attended the troops in the Field, as a surgeon during the late rebellion in that county, particularly at Tarah, where by his professional exertions many valuable lives were saved.
Fingal Capt Skreen Cav.
John Preston Capt Navan Cav.

A list of the rebel prisoners attended by Dr Neligan by order of Brig.-Gen. Merrick.

Date.	Name.	Suffering.
July 12.	D.Fogarty Fever.	Cured.
12.	M. Casey. Gunshot wounds of the breast.	Cured.
14.	M. Bush. Do the hip.	Cured.
20.	M Kavanagh. Six gunshot wounds in back.	Cured.
20.	T. Murphy. Fractures of skull and 23 other wounds.	Cured.
22.	D. Byrne. Abscess in head.	Cured.
22.	H. Lacey. Do of breast.	Cured.
25.	T. Purcell. Wound of head.	Cured.
26.	J. Purcell. Fever.	Cured.
28.	L. McDonnell. Fever.	Cured.
28.	P. Mooney. Fever.	Cured.
29.	W. Lord. Fever.	Cured.
29.	J. Early. Gunshot wounds to the neck.	Cured.
August 3.	D. Doyle. Fever.	Cured.
3.	B. Kavanagh. Rheumatism.	Cured.
5.	B. Doyle. Fever.	Cured.
5.	P. Fortune. Fever.	Cured.
6.	William Reilly. Gunshot wound of leg.	Cured.
6.	G. Nowlan. Do of shoulder.	Cured.
6.	P. Doherty. Bloody Flux.	Cured.
7.	P. Connor. Fever.	Cured.
8.	H. Madden. Do.	Cured.
8.	P. Sheron. Contusion of the breast.	Cured.
8.	D. Byrne. Do of the lyons.	Cured.

10.	J. Conway. Do of the shoulder.	Cured.
13.	G. Hopkins. Fever.	Cured.
13.	G. Kelly. Fever.	Cured.
14.	M. McDonnell. Fever.	Cured.
15.	G. Byrne. Quinsey.	Cured.
18.	C. Dempsey. Fever.	Cured.
18.	W. Reidy. Fever.	Cured.
20.	P. Finlan. Fever.	Cured.
22.	E. Reilly. Gunshot wound of the arm.	Cured.

Galway 17th February 1800.

I certify that Dr Neligan of Navan attended, with my knowledge and consent, the prisoners that were such or brought in wounded while I was stationed in that town and I verily believe it is a correct return of the patients submitted to his care.

Th Merrick

Brig Gen.

Syddan cemetery, where the Wexford rebel Coffey and his family are believed to be buried.

The Memorial on the site of the croppy grave at Lobinstown:

'Erected in 1898 by the people of Lobinstown
and Syddan to the memory of the gallant men
who fought and died for Ireland one
hundred years ago, some of whom were
buried at the foot of this hill in this spot.

All all are gone but still lives on
The fame of those who died
But true men like you men
Remember them with pride.

Far dearer the grave or the prison
Illumed by one patriot name
Than the trophies of all who have risen
On liberties ruin to fame.'

11

The Dead

While no official accounts exist, it would seem certain that over 1,000 and perhaps many more Wexfordmen died on the expedition into Meath. Most of them were buried where they fell, some only covered over in shallow graves by local people. In many cases these graves were subsequently marked by large stones being placed nearby in the lanes and hedgerows, and a tradition existed for many years, and in many areas, of whitewashing these stones to distinguish them and draw attention to their significance. This habit died out, unfortunately, and with the passing of time, many of the stones were moved or became overgrown and the burial places became forgotten.[1]

In the appendix to Kavanagh's *The Insurrection of '98* there is an account which includes details of the burying of a great number of the Wexford dead at Tara, but this account is so riddled with inaccuracies that little credence can be placed on it. One detail of the account which certainly does ring true, however, is in noting that, after the battles, large graves were made along the ditches and the bodies of the rebel dead were collected on carts and brought there for burial in these large communal graves. This practice is evidenced by the many locations in Meath, as well as in Wexford and other parts, where there is a record of such burials.

Until recent times the only location, where the burial places of those killed on the expedition into Meath were formally marked, was at Leinster Bridge, Clonard, where the memorial recorded the names of the sixteen Wexford men interred there.

In the late 1940s Garda Richard Murphy, based in Slane, together with some others gathered information and recorded the locations of a number of 'croppy' graves, as they were locally called, in County Meath. He also collected a great deal of history and local folk memory related to each of these resting places. We are greatly indebted to him for saving so much detail which, almost certainly, would have, by now, been lost, and to his son Peter Murphy, Blanchardstown, for very kindly providing, and permitting the use of, records reproduced in the following section. The following grave details are reproduced verbatim from R. Murphy's notes.

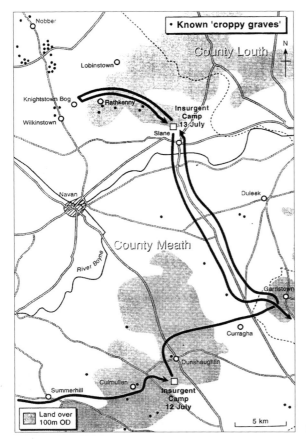

Map of the croppy graves.

Jim McDonald points out the stone marking the burial place of four Wexford 'croppies'. Beside the Nobber to Kingscourt Road at Whitewood.

Locations of rebel graves in and around County Meath.

Arodstown

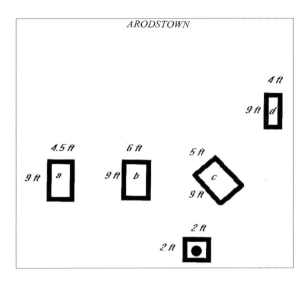

These graves are in a field belonging to Peter Brien. This field adjoins the old road between Arodstown and Culmullen. Mrs Mary Ann Lynch (87) heard old Tom Brien relating to her father about the graves. Mrs Mitchell's father died in 1887, aged about 79 years. Mrs Mitchell was previously married to a man named Lynch, her maiden name was Barry. Tom Brien was great grandfather to the present occupier Peter Brien.

Her story is that, in the morning time, a very big crowd came up the field outside northwards – came from Mr Shannon's field. They were very tired, wounded, hungry and exhausted – they were barely able to crawl – does not know where the battle was. Tom Brien's father, Dominic, had plenty of potatoes, oats and milk and fed them, but they died there – they were all buried in those graves and they came from Wexford as people all around said afterwards – she did not listen to all the conversation and regrets now that she walked away and did not take much interest in the two men's conversation.

(The spot *e* may indicate the spot where a man was executed) - remainder missing. Another grave on the other side of the fence almost parallel with *d* – a grave 7ft by 4ft.

Jenkinstown Bridge

Is on the road between Summerhill and Dunboyne – the branch road towards Kilcloon. One grave 6ft by 4ft (N/S) and lies on the roadside between end of wall over bridge and the crab tree. The grave was under an old crab tree since disappeared. Michael Dunne relates the following which he heard from Eliza Doyle, who was 91 years of age (dead over 30 years) – 'Two were buried at the old crab tree, one was a woman, they were coming from Gaulstown direction'.

Curraghtown

On the road between Culmullen and Mullagh cross, in Dick Leonard's field, at the entrance to the Point to Point races, in the corner on the left hand side. Two graves (a) 15ft by 4ft, alongside the fence (E/W) and (b) 6ft by 5ft —some stones on top of this.

John Lee (78), Culmullen, told us about these – also Edward Smith of Woodtown, who said this field was in wheat in '98 and the croppies were hiding in it – some years ago bones were found near the surface on grave (b). Mr Leonard's workmen intended to put a gate in the corner and, on account of the bones, decided otherwise. An old road ran along this fence towards Gaulstown.

Edward Smith also related that the rebels divided at Madden's Cross coming from Clonard – some went towards Tara and others towards Garristown – both parties avoided Dunshaughlin – the leader was mounted on a horse – the yeomen pursued them from Clonard and ambushed them between Culmullen and Mullagh Cross.

Gaulstown

One grave on roadside a few yards south of ash tree with cross on the side of the road. 6ft by 4ft. This is the road from Doolins to Gaulstown. John Lee, Culmullen, said there used to be a heap of stones on the grave – a Wexford straggler wounded died here after escaping from Lawless's barn. A man named Bruton, since dead, used to renew the cross on the tree.

Gaulstown

A short distance further on (from the previous grave mentioned) there is a large grave, 21ft long by 4.5ft in the corner of field, left-hand side and near the little bridge. The land is owned by Mr Delaney, Batterstown. John Lee says there were 21 rebels caught in Lawless's barn – two fields to the right – and executed. Lee pointed out the tree where they were executed. It is on a fence W of the barn a field away. Mr D. McCarthy divined the spot where they fell. John Lee says that he and his father levelled the barn about the year 1900 – one day while at this work a stranger called and said, 'You are levelling the barn where the Wexford men were hiding in '98 and from which they were brought out and executed'. Then he asked, 'Where is the big tree of Gaulstown?. The men were executed there.' Lee says he got a hatchet for the stranger and chopped off a bit of the tree as he knew the rebels were executed there. Lee says the barn was on the road side of the big elm tree and near it, in the middle of the field where the ruins of an old house are.

The Lawlesses used to bring hay to the market in Dublin – the name was seen on the carts and so was unwelcome in the city. Alic Hynes (73) heard his mother (died 1942) say the Wexford men took shelter in a barn of Lawless's. Mrs Hynes heard this from Mrs Fitzpatrick, who lived down the lane opposite Lawless's – also related that a girl in Lawless's house, who could speak Irish, gave the Wexford men a hint that the Lawlesses had sent for the yeomen at Dunshaughlin or Dunsany or Killeen or Trim. The Wexford men scattered, three were caught hiding under the little bridge in Gaulstown (near the grave) they were executed and buried outside in Mr Delaney's field – Mr Delaney lives at Portane, Batterstown. 'The spot was pointed out to me' she said.

Michael Dunne says most of the Wexford men, who got out of the barn, hid in a field of corn where the barn was – some were shot in this field – others executed at the ash tree – Fingal's Yeoman came in over McKeevers Hill, Bogganstown, at the back of Lawless's along the river from Culmullen side – the locality known as the Fassanagh – Miss Doyle says it got the name in '98 – Lawless's of Fassanagh – the name of Lawless is one of opprobrium in Co. Wexford – the yeoman camped in a field near Leonard's known as 'the camp field'.

Rathkenny

Single grave 6ft by 4ft on the road between Slane and College Hill – it lies, on the left, at Capt. Dean's wall – a large stone indicates it and the grave lies on the College Hill side of it. Evidently this stone was placed at the head of the grave.

Perhaps it is this grave Countess of Fingall refers in 'Seventy Years Young' page 108, 'Beside the road there Croppie's stone erected after '98, to mark the place where the croppies, or rebels, were buried. Below it there is a little old burial ground where the Flemings of Slane used to be laid at the end of their days'.

Horistown

Three graves on the esker on the Slane/Rathkenny road right-hand side.

(a)   15ft by 6ft N/S
(b)   6ft by 4ft E/W
(c)   9ft by 6ft N/S

This part of the roadside is in the townland of Horistown – the townlands of Dreminstown and Mt Eivirs join the fence. Local tradition, which is very strong, relates the croppies graves are here. There are stones heaped on grave (a) which runs along the roadside. (b) grave is beside the fence (alders). Perhaps all bodies are lying in grave (b) E/W.

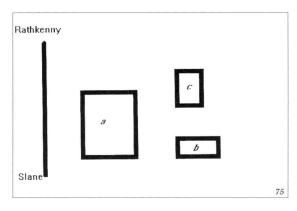

75

Rathkenny

On the roadside Rathkenny church – Post Office. One grave 6ft by 4ft. 30 yards beyond the turn – road leading to Parsonstown on left side.

Creenwood

One grave on roadside – left – about 100 yards the Slane side of Creenwood school. 12ft by 5.5ft. More accurate location – one yard Slane side of first ash tree with ivy and extends in that direction 12ft. One grave 6.5ft by 4ft in the field outside left beside the river – this is marked with a loose slab on which there is a cross – this stone lies on the centre of the grave N/S.

Knightstown

On the hill, where site of old school, we located seven graves.

(a)   Grave against the wall (south) the dimensions already marked with loose stones 18ft by 7ft.
(b)   All the area covered by the old schoolhouse.
(c)   6ft by 4ft.
(d)   7ft by 4ft N/S.
(e)   6ft by 4ft near old stump.
(f)   28ft by 6ft E/W.
(g)   18ft by 4ft.

(a)   Grave on roadside Navan side of Callaghan's house. 30ft by 6ft. It is about 30 yards from Callaghan's same side. Large elm tree 6 yards towards Callaghan's begins the grave.
(b)   One grave 6ft by 4ft between big stone and young ash tree about 150 yards from Callaghan's.

Author's Note: It may not be clear from the above whether (a) and (b) mentioned in the first part relate to the (a) and (b) immediately above, but it would certainly appear that they are quite separate sites.

Stephenstown/Headstown Road

In field in from Lorcanstown road.
(a)   One grave at gap 6ft by 4ft. The gap is filled with stones over the grave one foot of which extends into the field now owned by the Church body.
(b)   Another grave in the gateway opposite in the direction of the fort and leading into the field in which the fort is situated. 6ft by 4ft. John Larkin, who lives near, says there were brass buttons found in the grave.
(c)   That there was an old passway through these fields to Castletown.

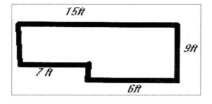
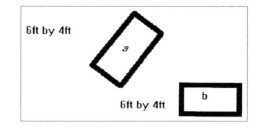

Herdstown

On the road leading up to the old road in Joseph Curran's field – on the right where there was a wood two graves. These graves are roughly marked by big stones. On left-hand side of road in John Kane's field on the side of the fort there is one grave 6ft by 4ft E/W on east side. Christopher Roarke gave the information about these graves to his son Phil Roarke now living in Spiddal, Nobber. The father died in 1921 aged 91 years.

Along old road – Headstown.

(a)   After entering the field first grave is about ten yards from the gate and a big stone marks it – because of briars difficult to get dimensions of area.

(b)   Sixteen yards further on, grave 6ft by 4ft where clay fell down under old bush.

(c)   Further on, westwards grave 6ft by 4ft – it faces out N/S – a slab in the form of a cross marks it, '98 inscribed.

(d)   Further on, in field on right – the fence running at right angles – cut away wood – grave 15ft long –dimensions shown on diagram. Three big stones mark it. Starts one yard S of Sycamore tree.

(e)   Further northwards under this fence grave 24ft by 9ft. Between two stones – over the grave big clump of briars.

(f)   About 100 yards over eastwards a single grave 6ft by 3ft – a big stone marks it – grave N of this.

Cavin Hill Raffan

Up road behind Carry's cottage and in the first gateway on left – turn right and grave commences at first big stone.

(a)   Grave 30ft by 4ft then there is a break of 12 ft and

(b)   grave commences 6ft by 4ft.

(c)   Proceed across field south-west direction and into next field to ruins of old house – Fr Conlon's. In the dyke or boreen there is a grave 14ft by 6ft. The end of the grave is marked by a big stone and it runs its distance from that towards Navan. Off road from Cavin Hill to Rahood – enter gate opposite Cumiskey's cottage and across long field towards end right-hand corner – enter narrow cut-away wood. One grave here 6ft by 4ft.

Mr Faulkner owns the land.

Thomas Cummiskey (90) a few years dead related the place of burial – somewhere in the wood. He said a wounded croppy went to the well in the field you cross for a drink and died beside it – his body was conveyed for burial to the wood. This well although a good distance is still used by the Cummiskeys.

Rahood

This side of entrance gate to Rahood Ho. Big grave on roadside right. 38ft by 6ft. An old bush stands about in centre of grave. E/W. A stone marks the end W. Mr McCarthy found spot in centre of road where the bodies dropped – big ash tree there still –the gallows branch broken off – trace of it to be seen.

Muff – Nobber

Half mile N. of Nobber in field on left noticeable as big heap grave 19ft by 7ft. Tradition says those were executed in the wood further on on the hill. Mr McCarthy found spot where bodies dropped off tree still standing outside fence on left beyond tillage field. George Eoghan knows the particular spot. The rod indicates a spot circular, about 2ft in diameter.

Bellew

On roadside on left between Lynch's cottage and Charles' – esker on road – grave 21.5ft by 6ft.

Duleek the Deans

On roadside between Gaskinstown Road and The Deans left. Grave 21ft by 4ft. McKevitt often heard of the Wexford rebels being caught at The Deans and executed. He quoted Thomas Courtney, who died in 1923 aged about 87, six or seven rebels were hiding in a barn beside where Frank McGrane now lives – they were there for three days and fed secretly – a servant girl gave them away – the soldiers came but did not find them – a soldier put a long bayonet up through the sally loft – it stuck in the foot of a rebel and he shouted – some rushing out through the window were shot – others hanged on a bush which fell in recent years – no one ever dared touch the bush – the mother of a boy who was shot came some time afterwards and found a sow of Morgan's eating the body in a field – she cursed the place – and all who lived in that place since never got on well – Morgan lived in it then.

Those names remain at The Deans – the Croppy field – the Croppy thorn – the Croppy wood.

More detail given by McKevitt about rebels at The Deans – small group of Wexford men on the run called to Morgan's, asked for food which they got and were put to sleep on loft of wicker sallies in the barn. He then informed Capt. Dillon of Mannastown, Ardcath – a commander of local yeoman – the latter arrived when the men were asleep and bayoneted them up through the loft and killed all but one – this one jumped out a window and was escaping across an adjoining field – fired on by yeomen who shot him in the belly – this young man was about twenty years old and over 6ft in height – he jumped 20ft when wounded before falling – they finished him with bayonets – a week after his widowed mother came looking for him and found his dead and mangled body in the field being torn by a sow of Morgan's – she cursed Morgan and his place and the curse remains to this day.

Morgan died insane – succeeded by Cooper, a wealthy man of Cooper's Hill – lost all – cut his throat – Mooney next – fail and went mad – next Kelly – did no good and drank heavily – his daughter married a Cromwell who died. This widow married the present occupier – he brought in £750 to the place well stocked – already he has sold half the farm.

Brownstown
One grave near Mr Macken's place on the left bank of the deep cutting looking at it from the road. The grave is heaped up as a result of earth thrown on it from the cutting. There is a cutaway wood here. The grave is 6ft by 4ft. Christopher Fagan (72) Kentstown, heard many old people speak of it. He actually pointed out almost the exact spot as it was shown to him – McLoughlins he says used to live here. His story is that a wanderer – rebel coming from Tara hid here – information was given to Tandy Taylor who came and shot the rebel. Taylor lived at Bellew near where the Charles's live now – Mooneys have the place now – the house is down – about thirty acres of land were attached to it – the house was on Mooney's side opposite J.J.Finegans – Taylor is supposed to have said, 'If anyone asks who shot him say Tandy Taylor shot him.' A Miss Taylor lived where Pat Mackin now lives and was a relative of Tandy Taylor's.

Deans
A single grave situated on right on the little hill beyond Dean's well – a big stone is on the centre of the grave – the grave runs along the roadside E/W – it is 6ft by 3ft. Mr McCarthy located a place of execution near the old thorn bush where tradition says the croppies were executed – in the field E of famous old barn. This old thorn bush was sacrosanct – no one dare interfere with it – time alone brought decay – a piece of the original is still there and an offshoot is standing coming from the original root.

Rathcairne Hill
This is about 1.5 miles north of Nobber – take turn to right off main Nobber/Kingscourt road at Gallons Hill. There is a big grave on the summit of this hill, roughly marked by stones – it is 18ft by 11ft extending N/S.

Marlstown
Off the road coming from Nobber-Kells towards Raffan. Two fields in, in a corner near old boggy patch the grave is 15ft by 6ft N/S about 5 yards from the hedge (W) and ten yards from the water edge where the bog commences. Phil Galligan told us about this grave.

Georges Cross

There is a grave on the old road behind the Garda Station, and convenient to the garden attached. Two big stones embedded in the earth mark the S/W end of the grave which is 6ft by 4ft and extending N/E. It is on Mr Pollock's land. Miss Casey, Clooney, says that the priest killed at Drakestown bridge was buried here. She heard from old Henry Cudden, Cross Guns. At the bridge itself, the rod dipped on a slender patch, stretching from the wall opposite the stone with the cross recently cut on it and '98. There is a widespread tradition in the locality that a Fr Murphy from Wexford was killed here. His blood was supposed to be on a small stone in the centre of the wall, and a vacancy left is still there.

Grange, Cross Guns

These graves lie near a broken down fence between Drakestown Bridge and Cross Guns. The land belonged to the late Patrick Kelly and Patrick Philips is the present owner. The fence runs northward from the old mound.
(a)   This grave 12ft by 6ft is well raised on top and shows the outline very well.
(b)   One yard further on, well raised on top like (a) is 12ft by 6ft.
(c)   One yard further on, centre portion slightly raised above level of ground is 6ft.
(d)   Some yards further on is another grave around which are many stones, some fixed in the earth and some loose. Beside it there is a used gap. The grave is 10ft by 8ft.
(e)   Some yards further on is a grave 6ft by 4ft – a big stone fixed in the earth marks the far end (north) of the grave.

All five graves are in a line the west side of the fence and extend S/N.

Dunshaughlin

On the Drumree – Dunsany road leading from Dunshaughlin at entrance of first lane on left – grave 15ft by 6ft N/S.

Culmullen

Sandpit in Mr Leonard's land, Culmullen, grave 12ft by 6ft at disused end, i.e. the southern end towards Summerhill. Grave runs N/S.

Killeen and Dunsany

Grave 18ft by 6ft on right side of road towards Dunsany crossroads, between the entrance gate to Dunsany and the lodge E/W a sharp stone at W end marks that end of grave.
The old hanging tree referred to by Lady Fingal in '70 Years Young' – the stump still remains some yards onwards towards the crossroads same side of the road – 46 yards onwards from grave. 'The Drop' was located 7ft from centre of stump in the direction of Dunsany crossroads.

Baytown

At Wainstown Cross which is about 500 yards the Summerhill side of Baytown Cross, a grave 9ft by 6ft: on right near side as one faces Dublin. A grave 6ft by 3ft situated 30

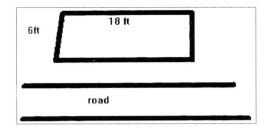

yards beyond Mr Paddy Barry's gate on right side. It is easily discernable, as the surface is raised above grave.

Irishtown Cross

About 60 yards Timoole side of this cross left. Grave 6ft by 4ft. Thomas Langan, Rathfeigh, says he heard that there are three bodies buried in the grave. McKevitt says they all referred to it as the Croppies Grave when passing. Local tradition has no doubt about it. The tree on which they were hanged was over the grave and fell with the big wind in 1903.

The dedicated research of Garda Murphy, carried out over a long period and over an area which included all of County Meath and, indeed, beyond has preserved much of the tradition and folk memory of 1798. The evidence, including his own account of the work, indicates clearly that a great many of his records are either lost or still undiscovered and include, perhaps, the location of many other grave sites.

In 1998 commemoration committees were formed (see 'Commemoration' in Appendice)] and much detailed work was done by them in investigating and confirming the burial places in their districts. Groups in Culmullen and Rathkenny areas listed and marked croppy graves, a very worthy undertaking which perpetuates the knowledge of these locations throughout Meath. Drawing on Garda Murphy's records and using other local knowledge a map of the grave locations was created.

In the Culmullen district the committee identified twenty graves at thirteen locations: 1, 2 and 3. Arrodstown – off the old coach road to Culmullen. These graves are on the lands of the O'Brien family who are direct descendants of the landowners in 1798. There are four graves for up to forty people.

4. This grave is 12ft by 6ft in Leonard's Sandpits. Large grave for unknown number.
5. Outside the east wall of the old Culmullen cemetery. Unknown number.
6. Curraghtown. Two graves, one 15ft by 4ft, the other smaller, 6ft by 4ft. This field was in wheat in 1798 and the croppies were hiding in it. An old road ran along the fence and is reputed to be one of the five roads running from Tara. The smaller grave may be for a yeoman killed at the scene.
7. Curraghtown. Three graves in a field alongside the modern laneway. These graves were probably for rebels who escaped from the barn of Gaulstown and were hunted down.

8. Curraghtown. One grave on the bank. Unknown number.
9. Gaulstown. One grave on the roadside 6ft by 4ft. A Wexford man died here. The site used to be marked by a cross carved in an ash tree.

Another large grave 21ft x 4.5ft for approximately eleven men who were hiding in the barn and were probably trying to make their way back to Wexford. Local tradition also relates that they had killed their own horses in Barrington's shed about three fields away. This would indicate that they were travelling by night and trying to evade the pursuing yeomen by day. Lord Fingall's cavalry came over McKeever's Hill along the river, the area known as the Fassanagh. On the arrival of the cavalry the rebels scattered, some hid in a field of corn beside the barn, some were shot in this field, others made it as far as Curraghtown or were killed in Downes' bog. Three were caught under the bridge at the road. In one field, south-west of the barn, is a large ash tree known as the, 'Big tree of Gaulstown', huge by any standards – 36ft in circumference at its base. It is now rotten but still has a few green shoots every year. On this tree some of the rebels were hanged.

10. Jenkinstown Bridge. One grave 6ft by 4ft and lies on the roadside twenty yards up the Kilcloon road, beside the crab tree. Two are reported to be buried here, one a woman. They were coming from Gaulstown.
11. Lismahon. Site known as the Monument Bush and was also the site of the 'Mass Rock' in penal times. Large grave for unknown number. During the widening of the road in the thirties some bodies were uncovered and re-interred in Rathregan cemetery.
12. Readsland. On the Drumree road from Dunshaughlin opposite Mickey Kenny's. Large grave 15ft by 6ft probably for rebels killed at Tara.
13. Killeen. Large grave 18ft by 6ft about 50 yards east of site of hanging tree. Again probably for those killed at Battle of Tara.
14. Downes' Bog. This site was marked by a stone with '98' inscribed on it. Also 'BG'- could be Bill Goodwin.
15. Wainstown Cross. Grave 9ft by 6ft now, due to road widening, under the road. Others killed here may be buried in Ballymacglasson Graveyard. A shed adjacent to the site in O'Toole's farmyard is also supposed to be the spot where two rebels were hanged.
16. Baytown Cross. A grave 6ft x 3ft, 30 yards beyond Mr P. Barry's gates on the right hand side towards Dunboyne.
17. Hill of Glane. A large grave on top of the hill with a big ash tree growing on the site. Probably rebels killed on return from Tara.
18. Marmions Gardens. Upwards of thirty rebels reputed to be buried here. After the Battle of Tara, skirmishes between retreating rebels and various yeomen took place in the bog near the road. Some of the fallen probably buried here.
19. Ballymaglasson. Unknown number buried here.
20. Rathregan. Unknown number buried here. Two rebels hanged in barn beside pub in village.

In Rathkenny the local committee identified and marked a number of graves at Miller's Hill, Big Wood, Creewood, near Rathkenny Church and at Slanecastle. The grave sites were commemorated by the erection of metal crosses, and a map of the sites was erected at the road junction near to the Roman Catholic church in Rathkenny.

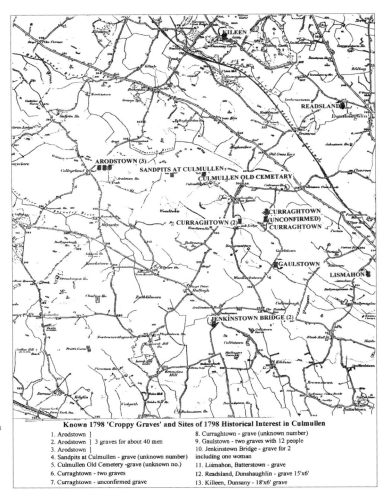

Known 1798 'Croppy Graves' and Sites of 1798 Historical Interest in Culmullen

1. Arodstown]
2. Arodstown] 3 graves for about 40 men
3. Arodstown]
4. Sandpits at Culmullen - grave (unknown number)
5. Culmullen Old Cemetery -grave (unknown no.)
6. Curraghtown - two graves
7. Curraghtown - unconfirmed grave
8. Curraghtown - grave (unknown number)
9. Gaulstown - two graves with 12 people
10. Jenkinstown Bridge - grave for 2 including one woman
11. Lismahon, Batterstown - grave
12. Readsland, Dunshaughlin - grave 15'x6'
13. Killeen, Dunsany - 18'x6' grave

Gravesites in Culmullen area identified and marked by the local commemoration committee in 1998.

A Final Word from the Author

Growing up in Wexford, before the television era and an ever-shrinking universe robbed whole generations of a rich oral tradition, I remember well the constant talk of times past in our house in St John's Road. My grandparents seemed to relish their role, as if it were their natural responsibility, to talk of other times – not just of the experiences of their own lives, but stories they, in turn, had heard from and through their grandparents. It was the same then, indeed, in families throughout the nation.

I recall two central topics in these discussions: Wexford's great seafaring tradition, sailors and ships and all their comings and goings – and '98.

The '98 rebellion was spoken of as if it had happened only the year before, and there was a pride in the talk of the heroism and suffering of the men who established the Wexford Republic, and the army of 25,000 Wexfordmen who fought to maintain it. In houses throughout the county, from Craanford to Carne, people spoke of what had happened in their townland or parish and knew the names and details, and relationships, of those involved. Where their own had taken part there was a particular pride and, with so many in the fight, almost all of County Wexford ancestry would have had connections with the insurrection, whether they knew it or not.

I remember being told of men, from the town, who had died at Forth Mountain and Vinegar Hill, being brought to Carrig for burial, of the fight for Ross and details of the terrible suffering throughout the whole of Wexford in the months following the rebellion. But the one aspect, which I never recall being talked about, was the army who marched away to Meath. Reading afterwards of the insurrection I found that most histories treated the event almost as an afterthought, a detail which had to be mentioned, peripherally, in order to complete the story but without giving any great significance to the incident.

The army of 6-7,000 Wexfordmen which marched over the Wicklow border, in the first week of July 1798, never to return except, in some cases, as individuals or small groups, does not hold a very strong place in the Wexford folk memory of '98. Why it should be so is not easily explained but, even soon after the rebellion, it was spoken of as something which had happened far away and beyond the immediate interest of those who were left – as, indeed, it had in the relative values of the time. There are many references to men who marched away with the army 'to the Boyne' or to those who 'escaped and returned home from the Boyne' as if it were a thousand miles away.

But we must pose the question, who were these much-forgotten people who went away to County Meath? When thinking of armies there is a natural tendency to see them as large anonymous bodies, without being able to look a little deeper and see them as consisting of many individuals, varied in their characteristics, backgrounds and motives.

This Wexford army would have been mostly made up of young men of fighting age, between sixteen and thirty-six years old – the kind of lads who might, in later years, have hurled with Oulart, Rathnure or the Faythe Harriers. There would have been farmer's sons or farm labourers from Monaseed or The Ballagh, apprentices or tradesmen from the towns – carpenters, thatchers, cobblers and smiths. Amongst them there might have been some known for their prowess as musicians – pipers or fiddlers – sportsmen or singers. They were all, individually, men of some importance, if only amongst their own circle of friends and relatives.

Marching wearily along the unfamiliar, dusty roads of Meath were, surely, men who had just a few months earlier, walked behind a horse and plough in a Wexford field, just as surely as there were those who had broadcast seed in the farmlands of Shelmalier early in that spring and who were to die in the ripening wheatfields of County Meath.

Even the names we know speak of Wexford, for they are there plenty to the present day. There were Dorans and Murphys and Rochforts and Sinnotts, Doyles and Kavanaghs, Byrnes and Laceys and Redmonds, each leaving a family somewhere, now, alas, forgotton with the passing of time, were brothers and sisters, parents and, perhaps, children.

There can be little doubt, as seen with the great advantage of hindsight, that the tactic of leaving County Wicklow and marching into Meath was an appallingly bad one in military terms for it achieved nothing other than the deaths of many brave men. Had the decision at Whelp Rock been to stay in Wicklow, it would surely have ended in a negotiated surrender on terms, as the Kildare leaders arranged on 21 July, or as the Wicklowmen did at Glenmalure four days later.

But we must not be too quick in our judgement of the Wexford leaders. Though they had learned much in the cauldron of the previous weeks, most were new to military matters and inexperienced in the tactics of war. They found themselves in a precarious position, surrounded on all sides by an enemy growing stronger by the day while they grew weaker, short of all the necessities for maintaining a campaign, of food, shelter and the materials of war. They had little good intelligence of what was happening elsewhere, rumour being the staple of whatever little information that reached them, and were acting without any clear options. They faced the stark choice between surrender and battle and it must be a tribute to their courage and indomitable spirit that the chose to fight on to the end.

The men who marched away from Sleedagh, before the dawn broke on that Friday morning of 22 June, were to march more than 500 miles, through eight counties of Leinster, before making their last stand at Ballyboughill three weeks later. They were patriots who 'rose in dark and evil days' to seek liberty and to end the tyranny and oppression of their time. Given the divergence of ancestry over a span of 200 years, those of us with a Wexford background will have had some family connection with one, at least, of the men of that army.

Whatever faults they may have had, it can surely be said of them that they fought bravely and were loyal to the end. Many of them left their young bones in the fields and along the roadsides of county Meath.

They deserve to be remembered.

Eamon Doyle

Appendix 1

The Wexford Rebels of '98 in the Folk Memory of County Meath

We are very fortunate indeed that, until very recent times, such a strong adherence to oral tradition and storytelling was part of the fabric of the everyday life throughout the country. Though now being rapidly silenced by the presence of television and modern technology, the tradition of passing on stories of times past, around winter firesides or in summer meadows, preserved much which might otherwise have been lost to us forever. In the main, the storytellers did not concern themselves with the great events of history but, rather, with local lore or family memories which brought alive the detail and colour of the way that life as it was then lived by the common people of Ireland, small stories that remained unrecorded in the annals of their times but which had an importance and significance in the family or parish in which they occurred.

Much of the knowledge passed down to us orally through many generations has become diluted through time and, though often clearly generated by some real event, the story, as now related, cannot be relied upon, uncorroborated, as an historical source. In many cases, however, where the events are of more recent times historically, a great deal of the information is of such detail, and from so many sources, that we find that the verity of the account is totally compelling and, given due care, can often be regarded as historically accurate.

During the time that I was researching the ill-fated march of the Wexford insurgents into County Meath in July of 1798, I found that the entire area of the Royal County had preserved a very strong folk memory of those times and that, with great good fortune, many of the memories of the older generation had been recorded in writing in the first half of the twentieth century.

The coming of the Wexford army and their battles in County Meath, followed by their dispersal over a wide area, must have been very traumatic for the local population and this is reflected in the way in which the details of their coming are still so vividly remembered and recalled. I found stories of Wexfordmen in every place along the line of their march, from Clonard in the south to Nobber, on the borders of County Cavan.

Willie Beatty of Ballindoolin, for instance, recalled for me the memory of the arrival of the Wexford army into the county on the morning of 11 July 1798. They came down the coach road to Clonard, he told me, and, 'they were mainly on foot but they had a good deal of horses with them'. He went on to say that it was noticed that, 'their clothes were in horrible bad conditition – some of them in rags'. This single detail seems to have made a lasting impression on people who saw them pass, and would be very understandable when we consider that these men had been marching and fighting for weeks, moving through fields and woods and sleeping rough in the open air.

The memory of the battle, which took place that day at Leinster Bridge, forms another major part of lore in that area. Graves of some the rebel dead were remembered locally and at one mass burial site people had preserved the names of the Wexfordmen, whose remains lay there, until they could be finally recorded on the memorial that was erected in 1898. These were Dowd, Kiernan, Rochford, Sinnott, Doyle, Redmond, Roach, Boland, Reilly, Doran, Nolan, Murphy, McCrath, Hore, Harpur and Hogan.

Nearby, I got the story of Jim Doyle from some of his direct descendents, the Doyles of Kinnegad and Jim O'Callaghan of Rathmines. Young Jim, then sixteen years old, hid after the Battle of Clonard in a potato field for two nights before he ventured out and sought help from local people. He was eventually sheltered by the Whytes of Aughamore and, after some years, married the daughter of the house. It is not clear how many children they had but at least two, William, who died on 18 June 1845 aged forty-two, and James, who passed away on 1 December 1847, aged twenty-nine, predeceased their father and are buried in Hardwood cemetery near Kinnegad. Jim, who was born somewhere in County Wexford in 1781, lived until about 1860 and was always known locally as 'The croppy'. He was an excellent farmer and was remembered as having introduced the practice of beekeeping to the area. He had many other skills, such as carpentry, and Jim O'Callaghan owns a fine chair which he made early in the nineteenth century, for use in his own household.

While the outcome seems to have been a happy one for Jim, one of the sadder stories was told to me by John Robinson of Kilrathmurray, who lives on the site of the Tyrrell house. John got the story handed down through his father, 'Some months after the battle, when things had died down, a widow woman came here from Wexford looking for her son. Her name was Roche.' John told me, and went on to say that she came in a pony and cart and the wheels were in such bad condition from the journey that local people had to repair them for her so that she could continue on her way. Again we find that it is the small, unusual, detail that is remembered which very often gives the story a ring of authenticity. John told me that he was told that the wheels of her cart were spokeless of a solid wooden type bound by iron rims.

Jasper Tyrrell of Ballinderry House told me of the history of his family and of how their house had been occupied on the nights of 10 July and 11 July by some of the

Wexfordmen. He brought home the reality of the event by showing me a small china dog, cracked down the middle and repaired. Written in pencil on the underside are the words, 'Broken during the rebellion of 1798'.

The Wexford rebels who had arrived in Meath on the evening of 10 July marched, after the battle at Clonard, up through County Meath during the following three days, 11 to 14 July 1798. They numbered at this time around 2,000 men, mainly mainly consisting of the remnants of the northern army of Wexford – men from the parishes east of the River Slaney. They were led north by Mogue Kearns, Anthony Perry and Esmonde Kyan with other leaders, very possibly including Thomas Dixon of Castlebridge. In military terms their position was hopeless as they were being hemmed in by increasing numbers of local militias and professional troops. Having fought their way almost to the Cavan border, they were forced into a one-sided battle at Knightstown Bog on Saturday morning, 14 July where they suffered a great number of casualties, having first been pounded by artillery fire. Many who tried to escape were hunted down and killed by the Northumberland Highlanders, but others managed to make good their escape. One large group on horseback, lead by Esmonde Kyan, managed to make their way back as far as Ballyboughill, in north County Dublin, later that evening where they were finally overcome.

It is the events of the aftermath of the battles which seem to have been remembered best in local lore, the stories of men who died and where they lay, of the hunt for the fugitives and the details of those 'croppies' who remained behind and lived out their lives in county Meath.

Noel Curtis of Creewood recalled for me a direct connection with that awful day at Knightstown Bog. He remembered being told by Johnny Reilly, who was at the time over ninety years old, in 1955 that his grandfather had told him that, as a boy, he had stood on the roadside and watched the Wexfordmen coming from the battle down the old Derry coach road:

They came down the road and passed me by, not all together, but in bunches, on horseback. The last groups were wounded or carrying wounded on their horses. One of these groups halted at a place opposite the old Creewood school and took down a wounded man who died almost immediately. They left his body by the roadside. This is the body which is buried in the adjoining field at Creewood, now owned by the Wall brothers, beside the little river.

The burial place was then marked by a flat stone bearing a symbol and, in the year 1998, a white steel cross was erected at the spot.

Some of the memories of old people in Meath were recorded, sometimes in considerable detail, by local historians. Fr John O'Reilly CC of Lobinstown collected a number in his parish in 1948 and, in many cases, the detail is so vivid as to almost bring the moment alive.

Ellen Quaile, born in the second half of the nineteenth century told him of the sad fate of two Wexfordmen on the day of the battle at Knightstown Bog:

My great grandfather was returning with lime from Ardee. He passed through Syddan – the only road to Ardee was through Syddan in those days. He said there was no one in Syddan or district when he passed through; all had fled as the Yeomen and Militia were said to be around. When he came to where Pat Corbally's cottage is he saw a man – a croppy – lying badly wounded. He stopped and went to his aid and spoke to him, but he could not answer as he was in dreadful condition and past human aid. He died soon afterwards. Another 'croppy' was found lying outside where Corbally's house now is – at the door. He was badly wounded but lived for a week hidden in the fields. The neighbours assisted him and gave him food, though they were scared of being discovered doing so. A Yeoman called Brinkley, who lived at Parsonstown, heard about his whereabouts and came with his men and shot him.

Mrs Quaile said that there was a third 'croppy' in the group and that they were all Wexfordmen. She did not know the fate of the third man.

Many of the stories collected from local people were about Wexfordmen who were hidden until the hue and cry died down and of some of those who remained on and, perhaps, married in County Meath. Fr O'Reilly wrote down some of these memories.

Mrs Geraghty of Killeary, who was ninety-seven years old when she recounted the story, told of a neighbour who hid a 'croppy' in a meal bin in the house for days after the fighting in the area.

John Kiely, born in 1867, told of a man named McEvoy who came from Wexford and who was hidden by the Smyths of Brownestown, when being pursued by the militia. He was later given work in the locality and eventually married a local girl. John Kiely recalled that he knew his daughter and his son named Owen McEvoy, when he, himself, was a young lad living in Rathbran Mor. He said that they are all buried in Rathkenny cemetery. A number of other parishoners also told the story of McEvoy, giving details of his descendants who were then still living in different parts of Meath.

One of the other insurgents who remained behind after the incursion into County Meath, and who appears to have left a lasting impression in the district, was John Coffey, who lived at Greenhills near Ardee. John Kiely was one of those who spoke of him to Fr O'Reilly.

Coffey was said to have been a schoolmaster from Wexford who married and brought up a family in Greenhills. He is buried, together with his son John and daughter Peg in Syddan graveyard.

A lot of people also knew and recounted the story of the Hackett brothers and the various accounts differ very little in the telling. They tell of four Wexford brothers named Hackett who marched with the insurgents into Meath. One was killed at the 'Battle of the Bridge' near Rathkenny on the day of the fight at Knightstown. The other three fought on and, after the battle, found a hiding place on the farm of a local family some miles away. When things had quietened a little, they managed to make their way home to their native Wexford. One of them, however, had fallen in love with the young daughter of the farmer who helped them, and promised her that he would be back. Within a year he made good his promise and returned and the pair married.

Their Hackett descendents lived in the area until the early 1900s, when it is thought they all went to America.

Where families such as the Hacketts are involved the oral traditions can usually be very easily authenticated. In the case of stories relating to individual events, however, it is sometimes a little more difficult to be certain which of the details have come down to us untainted by time and telling. In relative terms 1798 is a fairly recent historical event and, as late as the 1940s when many of the recollections were recorded, there were people still living who had, themselves, known participants or eyewitnesses to the events of that year. Some few of the stories had been passed on directly by witnesses to the old people interviewed or had come down to them through a single intermediary. Given the importance of oral tradition in those times and the fact that many of the accounts came down directly through families, and would surely have been recounted many times round their firesides, it is likely that, in general, the credibility of most of the accounts can be accepted.

Just beyond the Meath border in Ballyboughill, where the Wexfordmen made their last brave stand, the Swift family has lived, since the eighteenth century, and has passed down much of the history of the event through the family. Peter Swift recalled that on 14 July 1798, the remnant of the Wexford army first stopped at a place called the Murrough, Westpalstown, which is on the Oldtown side of Drissogue lane. Here they attempted a brief rearguard action against the pursuing cavalry. After the battle the Swift family sheltered two Wexfordmen one of whom was named Colfer, according to Peter. He also told the very interesting, and unusual, story of another rebel to be given help by local people in that area:

Watsons of Springhill hid a man from Wexford named Walsh, who stayed with them for eighteen months, until the hue and cry had died down when he returned to Wexford. Almost forty years later a priest came to minister in the parish of Oldtown and called on the Watson family. He introduced himself as Fr Walsh – a son of the rebel they had sheltered in '98.

In the same area, Sean McPhilbin of Westpalstown recalled the story of a young girl named O'Hagan, who was returning from Ballyboughill, along Drissogue lane, on the day of the battle. Hearing a commotion behind her on the road she ran and hid in the ditch just inside a field. A man carrying a pike rushed into the field, closely followed by two men on horseback who overtook him and circled him in the field. As each passed the pikeman faced the nearest of the yeomen and presented his pike in their direction. Then the two horsemen halted each on one side of the fugitive, drew their pistols, took careful aim and shot the rebel dead. It was a memory the little girl carried with her throughout her lifetime.

Further west in south Meath John Gavin of Knock, Killua, recalled the story he had been told about the Fagan family of Cloran. According to John, after the Battle of Knightstown Bog, it was the practice of the Navan Yeomanry to carry out sweeps of the country every day looking for fugitive rebels. On one occasion they came to Cloran, where a family named Fagan lived. The Fagans had five or six children, who were out playing on the road when they saw the horsemen coming, and they ran in, in fear, to tell their parents. The Yeomen dismounted and came into the house, probably looking for information. The Fagans could not give them any and, indeed, very probably did not know anything. The militiamen began to threaten the parents and became angry at getting no adequate response and, either to frighten the family into co-operation or to punish them, murdered two if the Fagan children. Descendents of the Fagan family are still living at Clonmore, Kildalkey. John Gavin also says that some of the 'croppies' are buried at Daingan, near Summerhill. The grave, he says, is in a field, on the right-hand side of the road as you veer to the right to go down the hill, after passing the entrance to the Daingan Castle. The graves are slightly raised but not marked in any way.

Another piece of valuable information from the same source relates to one of the Wexford men who remained in county Meath. John says:

> After the battle at Knightstown a man named Kelly was hiding in the Killallon/ Archerstown area, near Clonmellon, together with a number of others. They set out towards Tara but were ambushed by a party of Yeomanry between Fordestown and Girley, and a number of the rebels were killed, but Kelly managed somehow to escape. He returned to Archerstown and moved from house to house until the hue and cry died down. He lived out his life in the area, though he never married, and is buried in an unmarked grave in Archerstown graveyard.

Another source recalled that, later in his life, John Kelly was well known in the parish where he visited particular houses in the evenings to 'give out' the Rosary. His grave was finally marked in 1998 in Archertown cemetery with an appropriate plaque.

The capture and execution of fugitive rebels was also well remembered in local tradition and the versions vary very little in regard to a number of these events. One these which recalls the twenty-one Wexfordmen who took refuge in Lawless's barn near Gaulstown and has been recounted by many local people. One of them Alic Hynes recalled being told by his mother:

> The Wexford men took shelter in a barn of Lawless's. My mother was told this by Mrs Fitzpatrick, who lived at that time, down the lane opposite Lawless's..A servant girl in the house, who could speak Irish, gave the Wexford men a hint that the Lawlesses had sent for the Yeomen at Dunshaughlin and they scattered about the area. Three were caught hiding under the little bridge in Gaulstown – they were executed and buried outside in Mr. Delaney's field .The spot was pointed out to me.

In the days immediately following the collapse of the Wexford army as an organised force the search for individuals and groups of fugitives seems to have been carried out with enthusiastic ferocity, mainly by local yeomanry and militia. With some notable exceptions, particularly Lord Fingal's Cavalry who took many prisoners, the practice seems to have been to execute those captured on the spot. Many local people, at considerable personal risk, tried to help the Wexford rebels with food or hiding places, but a great many were captured and perished.

Thomas Courtney, who died in 1923 at the age of eighty-seven, told of:

six or seven rebels hiding in a barn at The Deans – beside where Frank McGrane now lives – they were there for three days and fed secretly until a servant girl gave them away. The soldiers came and could not find them – they had been put in a loft of wicker sallies. The soldiers were led by Captain Dillon of Mannastown, Ardcath. One of the soldiers put a long bayonet through the sally loft and it struck the foot of a rebel and he shouted out. Some of them rushed out of the window and were shot, others were hanged on a bush which fell in recent years. No one ever dared to touch the bush.

We are indebted, for the collection and preservation of the greatest number of accounts and grave sites, to Garda Richard Murphy.

Richard Murphy was born in Glenmore, County Kilkenny, in 1894 and joined the Garda Síochána in 1923. He served in Kilbeggan, Co. Westmeath, until 1929, when he moved to Killucan and then to Georges Cross, County Meath. In 1935, he transferred to Slane where he served until his retirement from the force in 1957. He died in 1991.

During his time in County Meath he was an enthusiastic collector of the accounts of 1798 as remembered by old people throughout the county and recorded much of the oral tradition of that time. In a letter, still extant, he mentions that he had, at the time of it's being written, interviewed, '151 old people ranging from Dunsany, two miles S.E. of Tara Hill to Kingscourt, Co. Cavan.' It is believed that he went on to interview many more, possibly as many as 300.

The whereabouts of his record of many of these interviews is still, sadly, undiscovered but his son, Peter Murphy of Blanchardstown, has in his possession fifty of the accounts, which he generously made available to me and which form the basis of the remaining accounts.

Traditional account of the croppies who were in Carrickdexter and Beaupark in 1798 given by John Gallagher, Slane, on 9 June 1950, to Guard R. Murphy, Slane.

I am 67 years of age and was born in Slane on 27th May, 1883. I knew old Mickey Southwell of Barristown, Slane, very well. He was 90 years of age when he died in 1948. I often heard him talk about the croppies in '98. He said that a large number were hiding in a ditch (a deep channel) on the north side of the river Boyne opposite Beaupark house at the time. There was a herd named Denis Rourke in the employment of Lambarts of Beaupark then. When this herd was on his rounds looking after the cattle in the evening he came across those croppies who were hiding in the deep ditch. He arranged to bring them across the Boyne that night. Some time later on that same night, or early the following morning, he rowed them across the river to the south side. When across, he brought them to his own house where he kept them for about two hours until they had taken some food. He then accompanied them for some distance and showed them the direction they were to take for Wexford. At that time Mr. Lambart was an officer in the local Yeomanry.

Some years afterwards Denis Rourke had occasion to go to Wexford on business affairs. He used to travel by a float drawn by two horses. As far as I can remember he was going to the residence of some gentleman, whose name I cannot remember, when something happened to the float. A crowd gathered, amongst whom were some of the men he had rowed across the Boyne at Beaupark in 1798. When they saw the name Lambart on the float they asked him some questions and, to their delight, they recognised him as the man who had befriended them. No sooner was this known than they took the horse from under the float and pulled it themselves into the next town (I think it was Gorey) and lavishly they dispensed with 'the cup that cheers.

The story of Denis Rourke bringing the Wexford men across the Boyne was so strong in local memory as to be compelling. Several who gave accounts to Garda Murphy told almost identical stories of the event, some with even greater detail. Hugh Morgan of Carrickdexter, for instance, who said that Rourke was a good friend of his family, says that he accompanied the Wexfordmen as far as the Hill of Skryne, while James White, of Rathdrinagh, says specifically that there were forty-eight rebels in the group helped by Denis Rourke.

There are a number of accounts of the Wexford rebels being aided by local people. In 1948, eighty-seven-year-old Michael Creegan of Faganstown recalled:

I am a labourer by occupation. I often heard my father (John Creegan) who was over 75 years when he died in 1890 say that there were three croppies or Wexfordmen hanged on Tankardstown Hill in 1798. They were captured by the Yeomen from Slane, who were under the command of one Captain Gettings, whose troops were then quartered where the Boyne Terrace now stands near Slane Bridge.

The bodies of the dead men were taken from the hill and were buried on the east river bank, in the late John Reilly's field and about two hundred yards south-west of Creewood National School.

Old Morris, the then occupant of Tankardstown Estate, would not allow them to be buried on his land. They received spiritual attention from Father Mulligan who was interrupted by Captain Gettings who said, 'hurry up with that business we have no time to be losing here'.

The priest replied saying that he would do his duty in spite of him and all the devils in Hell. When the priest had finished the three men were hanged from a triangle.

There was another Wexfordman buried in a field owned by Mick Reilly of Creewood. Another croppy was killed by the Yeomen at Gernonstown and buried in the Alt, [a Gaelic term used in north-east Meath to describe a ravine or narrow glen with a high cliff on one or both sides] at the lower end of Tommy Brien's third field and about four hundred yards south-west of the Slane/Rathkenny road. His grave is about twenty-five yards down the slope, in or about sixteen yards south-east of the sand-pit and about forty-five or fifty yards north-east of the stream or river running below it.

He was entertained the night before by a person named Russell who then resided convenient to where the Fowler Ginnity now lives. He left early the next morning but was surrounded by a troop of Yeomen on horseback and shot. His resting place is now covered by a clump of blackthorns.

There were three other Wexfordmen killed on the Deer-park and buried there not far from Rushwee Catholic Church. There is a heap of stones placed over them. During the search for those men it was said that a Protestant Yeoman saw them hiding in some ferns and brushwood but passed them by, until a Catholic Yeo came along, drew attention to them and had them shot.

Seven croppies were found hiding in some scrub and brushwood on the lands of one Mr. Kelch at Carrickdexter by the owner. He invited them to his house, gave them food and put them up in the barn for the night. Later that same night Kelch informed the Captain of the Yeomen at Slane that he had seven croppies secured in his barn. Gettings caused a gallows to be erected on the hill over the town at the quarry beside where Thomas Morgan now lives on the Slane-Drogheda road. When Father O'Hanlon, the local parish priest, became aware of the situation he interceded with Lord Conyngham who reprimanded Gettings for having erected a gallows on his estate without permission and prevented the execution of the prisoners.

Lord Conyngham took those Wexfordmen with him to the castle, and it was said that he gave them free passes to Wexford, and ordered the gallows erected on the hill to be taken down.

Creegan goes on to tell how a man named 'Tara' Kealy of Stackallen saved four men from Wexford who were hiding in a cornfield, which he was searching with other members of the yeomanry. When he discovered them he whispered to them to keep quiet and pretending that his part of the field had been searched thoroughly and that he had found nobody.

The coming of the rebel army made a very strong impression on the folklore of County Meath, particularly in the northern half of the county. The stories which told of the events of 1798 formed much of a very strong oral tradition, which persisted almost to the present day and, while in some cases details have become garbled with the passing of time and generations, nevertheless a great deal in the body of stories has a ring of authenticity and accuracy. In the case of many collected by Richard Murphy, sources reaching well back into the nineteenth century are given, and many of them are reinforced by other versions. Thus they form a valuable account of events, which should not be overlooked when examining the history of that time.

It is significant, perhaps, that most of the accounts pertain to the rebels from Wexford after the battle at Kinghtstown on 14 July 1798, when they had become dispersed into groups and individuals and were seeking to make good their escape and return to their homes. This is not at all surprising, for many hundreds of fugitives spread around the north County Meath, hiding where they could, seeking food and shelter whilst not knowing whom they could trust, and constantly being vigilant for those hunting them down, must surely have been traumatic for the entire population of the area.

Some of the recollections were of the finding of pike heads and other artefacts relating to the time while many others told of the burial sites. The tradition of marking the graves of the croppies is mentioned and this confirms the respect which the local people showed for the resting places of the dead and of how they ensured that the locations would not be forgotten. Nicholas Weldon, born in Higginstown in 1886, told of a grave site on the Slane/Collon road, 'His grave was covered over with a medium-sized heap of stones when I saw it first. My father used to tell me to throw a stone on this grave whenever he knew I was to pass that way.'

But, perhaps the most interesting and valuable, in many ways, are those accounts which mention the names and other details of the rebels who came to Meath in 1798. Joseph Everard of Rathdrinagh, born in 1879 in his account tells:

> In or about that time there was a Wexford croppy who got wounded in the shoulder by a pistol shot fired by one of the Yeomen commanded by Major Gorge. He succeeded in escaping from them and got into a kind of wood or large strong scrub at the south-east end of Rathdrinagh where he got clear of them and went into the house of a man named Madden. This man was a relative of my great-grandfather and then farmed a holding of about sixty-six Irish acres. The croppy remained with the Madden family for some time until his wound healed up and afterwards left for home. I never heard whether he got home safely or not. He was a young active lad. His name was Rowe and he was a Protestant.

William Downey, born at Sean-baile in July of 1874 stated that:

> Three Wexfordmen by the name of Feeley settled in Meath after 1798. Mickey lived at the bridge of Harlinstown, Lohey lived at Mullaghmore in Rathkenny, and the third, either Joe or Willie, lived at Donaghmore near Navan. They were wood-turners and all very tall men.

With regard to the same family, Patrick Wogan of Davidstown, born in 1888, recalled:

> I often heard old people say that Feeley's father or grandfather was one of the croppies who settled in Meath after '98. He originally came from somewhere near the Carlow and Wexford border. All the old Feeleys were remarkably tall big men. They were woodturners by trade and made butter-dishes, chairs, forms and other household articles.

The name of one of the rebels who did not survive is remembered by Thomas Connell of Cardrath, who was born in 1868:

> There was another Wexfordman buried in a field owned by a man named Reilly of Creewood. His name was Crawley. The field where he was buried is slightly north of the house where I was born.

It would appear that he became separated from the rest of his comrades when seen by three Yeomen on horseback. He was then in a field on the Tankardstown estate west of the road at the schoolhouse, and was followed immediately by the three Yeomen. The first horseman that reached him wheeled his horse to one side (apparently with the intention not to kill him) making out at the time that his horse had bolted. The next Yeoman came up and shot him. It would appear that he only received one shot. The wounded man managed to crawl as far as Connell's and asked for a drink which was given to him. He told them then that his name was Crawley.

Of course many of the recollections relate to rebels who managed to avoid capture and stayed on to live out their lives in County Meath. One of these was a man named Cavanagh. Patrick Carolan of Rathmore, Athboy, in recalling the stories he had heard about '98 from his father tells us:

At that time there was no public road running through this townland to Athboy. Rathmore was a most suitable place for men on the run in '98 because the turf bog at that period extended over a very large area. It was five miles long, and three miles wide; and was considered a safe retreat by the men evading enemy troops. Its area has been reduced very considerably since then due to reclamation.

Two of the three rebels that came here died and were buried in a field about forty perches at the Navan side of our house. I could not say whether they died from wounds or else. Although two croppies were supposed to have been buried in this field I am unable to point out their graves just because no one showed them to me. I often heard it said that on one occasion when the owner was going to plough this field, four strange men appeared to him one night and told him not to interfere with it. How true this may be I cannot say. One of them, named Cavanagh, survived and settled down here in Rathmore. He did not disclose his identity for some time until the country settled down. He posed as a travelling workman when he first came here. He later married a girl in the locality named Farrelly and brought up a family.

Michael Cavanagh, who resides in this townland, is a grandson of his.

A number of the accounts help to reinforce and authenticate information mentioned by others but, very often, it is the small additional details of significance which give a greater sense of the reality behind the stories. Michael Markey, for instance, born in Lobinstown in 1879, tells us of the Wexfordman, McEvoy, mentioned in Fr O'Reilly's memoir. He says that:

McEvoy lived for a while in '98 at Lynch's Cross. He escaped being captured by the Yoes, and later on moved further East towards Collon, and eventually settled down at Rathbranbeg, and brought up a family there. Old Nancy McEvoy was a daughter of his. She married Arthur Curry of Clougher many years ago. She would be an aunt of Sarah Doolan of Woodtown. Mrs Curry of Clougher had a family of four sons and one daughter. That daughter married Patrick Price of Knock, Castletown, and is the only survivor of that Curry family that I know of.

More details of the same McEvoy were given by seventy-four-year-old John Reilly of Clogher, Rathkenny, further helping to build up the story of this Wexford insurgent:

> A croppy by the name of McEvoy was sheltered by a family named Smith at Brownestown, near Kopkinstown, in '98. He was concealed behind and old cart which was lying against a wall of a hay-barn. He remained there, got married and settled down. He lived just beside where James Loughran of Rathbranbeg lived.

He goes on to give details the McEvoy family.

There is similar confirmation of other rebels who remained to live out their lives in County Meath. John Weldon of Mitchelstown talks about Coffey – said to have been a schoolmaster from Wexford, 'There was another croppy who was befriended by a Protestant family named Sillery, who then lived at Greenhills, Newtown, Creevagh. That Croppy's name was Coffey. He got married and settled down there for good. The last of his descendants was Peggy Coffey who died about forty years ago.'

Michael Biggy of Knock, who says he got his stories from his father, in giving us many interesting details of what happened in his area in 1798, includes a brief account of Joe Hackett:

> I heard tell of another Croppy named Joe Hackett. He escaped capture after the battle of Knightstown and got back safely to Wexford. He returned after some time and settled down at Wilkenstown, Co. Meath. My grandfather and old Joe Bradley knew him well. He wore a great big long flowing beard and used to walk down by Knock crossroads when going to Killary River to fish. He lived to be a very old man.

A final reference to one on the rebels by name comes in the recollections of Thomas Hickey of Ladyrath:

> There was a croppy kept here by my great-grandfather for over two years. I cannot remember exactly what his name was, but it was either Murtagh or Murphy. He was the heart's blood of a rebel. He was from Gorey. With the help of my great-grandfather and other local people he succeeded in getting back to Wexford. During his time here he slept in a kind of dug-out erected for him about one hundred yards north-east of this dwelling house. It was considered necessary at that time to take such precautions in order to evade capture should the Yeomen surround the place.

A great many of the accounts given to Richard Murphy detail the escape or killing of the insurgents, recalling the places in which they hid and of people who helped them to escape. Very little is recorded of the Wexford army prior to its dispersal, after the battle at Knightstown on 14 July. There is the occasional mention, however, which gives us a glimpse of the mayhem and perhaps panic, of the events of that day, when the rebel army ceased to be a cohesive and organised force, and broke into a great many groups and individuals, each seeking to escape the attention of the forces hunting them down without mercy. There were many minor skirmishes reported throughout the area. Ninety-three-year-old James Hoey of Carnacop, whose grandfather was an officer in the Yeomanry, tells us that:

> The Wexfordmen came from Raffin where a battle was fought between them and the Yeomen. After the battle they passed by at Crossguns, Stephenstown, Carnacop, Headstown, Fringerstown, towards Slane by Lobinstown. They were attacked by the Yeomen at Headstown and Fringerstown and some of them were killed there, and buried at the foot of Lobinstown Hill.

Thomas Carberry says that, according to his mother, Brigid Carberry, who died, aged ninety-two, in 1936, 'there were hundreds of them slaughtered in a battle which took place between those five very small hills, all of which are in the townland of Knightstown.'

Michael Biggy's account tells us:

> … a battle was fought in Knightstown bog between British troops and Wexford Croppies in 1798. The rebels were beaten and forced to retreat after losing many men. They retreated through Leggagh, on by George's crossroads, by Drakestown, to Raffin, where they fought another battle but were again beaten. After this battle the Croppies broke up into separate parties and went in different directions. Some of them went on towards Kilmainhamwood, others towards Nobber, more towards Woodtown and Ardee and Lobinstown. A lot of them were killed at Headstown and buried there.

There is one incident recalled by a number of people where a single Wexfordman with a 'long gun' delayed the advance of the pursuing troops until his colleagues had time to move on. All agree that this happened near Wilkenstown, on 14 July, and the story varies only slightly in the different recollections of the event. Some say that he was hiding behind a house, while others say a turf clamp, and there is a doubt regarding whether he was captured and executed or succeeded in escaping. Again, it is one of the memories which comes down to us with such conviction that it seems certain to have been based on a real incident. One version is that given in 1950 by Richard Lynn, aged seventy, who got the story from his grandmother, Alice Lynn, who died in 1902 at the age of eighty years:

> According to what they said the Wexfordmen came from the Navan direction. As the Insurgents advanced northwards they were followed by the Yeomen and other British Forces who had heavy guns. They were a considerable distance behind the rebels, and when they reached a certain point from which they could use the artillery on the retreating Insurgents, a Croppy was posted behind the house where Mrs Farrelly now

lives, with orders to fire on the advancing enemy troops in order to delay, and keep them in check, until his comrades had passed over Callaghan's Hill, and out of range of the heavy guns. When the British troops advanced to within a certain distance of Mrs Farrelly's house they were fired upon by the Croppy. They halted, examined the position of the house from a distance, but did not advance for a while due, perhaps, to expecting greater numbers of the rebels Rear Guard to have to contend with than were really there. When his comrades got over Callaghan's hill, he retired from his post, and safely overtook them north of Wilkenstown.

The collection of folk memories recorded by Murphy, are valuable, not just for the information which they give us of the events of the time, but for the colour which they add to those events. Many are clearly not the clinically accurate records which historians might prefer but, rather, constitute what the local people regarded as the most important and memorable events of that time or, perhaps, those which most closely effected their own families. The deep impression which the coming of the rebels from Wexford made on the people of the area permeates the accounts, and the sympathy and support for their cause is uniformly constant, even in those accounts credited to sources born in the first half of the nineteenth century. There is uniformity, also, in the people's perception of those characters who played a part locally in the events of the time. Gettings, the yeoman, finds no praise but Denis Rourke, who brought the rebels across the Boyne, is remembered kindly by a number of those who spoke. Another who is spoken well of by all is the liberal local magistrate, Mr John Pollock of Mountainstown. Several accounts record him as having protected those rebels found hiding in the district and Kate Rogers, born in Cloughree, Drumconrath, in 1884, tells us, 'I often heard it said that John Pollock of Mountainstown was very kind to any of the Insurgents who were lucky enough to approach him for his help in '98'.

Much of what has been collected here has been passed down the generations in meticulous detail, at a time when oral tradition was still a very important part of Irish rural life. It is well to finish with one of the accounts in full, which clearly brings out this attention given to detail in preserving the memories of '98:

Traditional account of five Croppies that were befriended at Commons, Slane, Co. Meath, in 1798, given by Thomas Cassidy at Knowth, on 6 February 1952, to Guard R. Murphy of Slane.

I am 49 years of age and was born at Commons, Slane, Co. Meath, in 1903. My father was 78 years of age when he died on the 19th November 1929.

I often heard him and John McGovern of Rathmaiden talk about the Croppies of 1798. According to what I remember them to say about those rebels, there were five Wexfordmen hiding in a field of oats near my old home in the townland of Commons. It was in the month of July of that year. My father often told me this same story but I did not take much interest in it at the time.

Those Croppies must have been in the corn for some time before being seen because they had a patch of it about the size of a large kitchen floor trampled down where they were eating the grain and lying down in it. This was in my great-grandfather's time.

Those men were bobbing up their heads now and again over the corn when seen by my great-grandfather and other people of the house. My ancestor and the other people present came to the conclusion that the men hiding in the corn were Croppies.

At that particular time it was considered most dangerous for either to harbour or befriend any rebels who had taken part in that rebellion. My great-grandfather went out to those men who were hiding in the corn. When he arrived at where they were, they asked him if they could trust him or was he going to inform on them. They further added that, if he was going to inform on them, they would go away immediately and try to get home as best they could. He assured them that he was not going to inform on them but would do his best to help them. He told them that it was most dangerous to attempt anything like that in daytime in case of being seen, as the Yeomen were patrolling the roads every hour, both by day and by night, but when night came he would try and get them across the Boyne. They were in a most terrible state for want of food. He went back to the house and returned with some food for them. They enquired of my great-grandfather as to how far they were from the River Boyne as they considered themselves safe once they got across it.

He brought them over to the house that night and gave them more food. When they had finished eating he brought them down through Littlewood, out through the land now owned by Thomas Robinson, across the Collon/Slane road at the Pound where John Cassidy's cottage now stands, across Stanley Hill to the old pump partly opposite the entrance gate to Jeanville avenue on the Slane/Drogheda road. When they got to the fence at this point they lay down behind a hedge and waited for a while to make sure whether or not there was anybody about before venturing across the road. They were only a few minutes there when they heard the noise of horses galloping in the direction of Slane, and to their surprise, a posse of Yeomen galloped by, towards Drogheda. The Croppies and my great-grandfather kept lying flat on the ground until all the horsemen had passed. They then ran across the road and through Johnston's field for the River Boyne.

My great-grandfather knew that there used to be a fishing boat at the Boyne not too far away. It was owned by a man named Morgan. This man then lived somewhere convenient to where the present loughhouse now stands at Rosnaree. This boat which usually be berthed at the South bank of the river happened to be at the North bank on this particular night when my great-grandfather and the five Croppies arrived at the place. The Croppies wanted him to go across the river with them in the boat and to bring it back again to the North bank. He told them that he knew nothing about using a boat on the water and so he did not go with them. They embraced him, bid him goodbye, and said that they would let him know when they got back home. He told them not to attempt to send him any message because it was too dangerous in case it became known that he had assisted them. If it afterwards transpired that he had befriended them it would mean destruction for him.

The five Croppies then got into the boat and rowed across to the South bank, tied it up there, and proceeded southwards. He never heard afterwards whether these men ever got home safely or not.

Although my great-grandfather assisted those Wexford-men to get away, he was in dread of his life in case it leaked out for the country was reeking with spies at the time. It was afterwards discovered that the boat had been used by some-one that night and, as a result, the whole place all around was searched by the Yeomen without finding anyone.

When our old dwelling house at Commons was being renovated in 1910, a '98 pike was found in the old thatched roof. It had a blade about 9ins long, and a hook on one side of it, with a socket about 4ins or 5ins long for a handle. It might have some connection with the five Croppies that were there in July 1798.

I often heard it said that a man named Rourke, who was either a Herd or Steward employed by Lambart of Beaupark, in '98 ferried a lot of Wexford-men across the River Boyne at Beaupark, in that year.

From what I heard my father say about the rebellion in '98 it would appear that the Wexford-men were not welcome to Meath as this County had just settled down after the rising at Tara, when those Croppies came along and started the trouble over again.

When a boy I heard old Willie Roche (locally known as the 'Butt of Oak') who lived in the hollow at Grangegeeth say that there was a Croppy buried under the grass margin on the west side of the road, slightly north of Fleming's gravel pit, in that townland in 1798; but I never heard what his name was. I also heard him say that there were two Croppies killed and buried somewhere near the little bridge on the Grangegeeth/Creewood road, beside Gargan's cottage at Crossanne, at that period. I was never shown their graves and, therefore, could not point them out.

Thomas F. Cassidy.
February 6th 1952.

The Tyrrell House at Ballinderry which was occupied by the rebels on the night of 10/11 July 1798.

Mr and Mrs Waltup (*née* Tyrrell) of USA with a pair of china dogs from Ballinderry House, one of which was broken and repaired. Written underneath is, 'broken during the rebellion of 1798.'

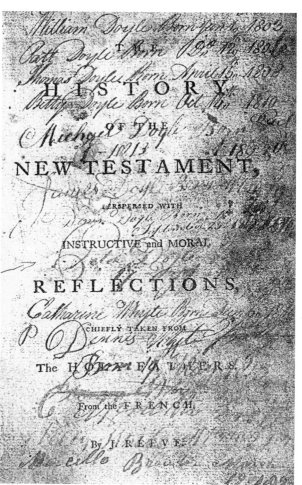

One of the surviving rebels whose story, best remembered and documented, is Jim Doyle. Jim, as a sixteen-year-old rebel at Clonard, hid for two days in a potato field before finding shelter, and work, at the house of Whytes of Aughamore. He married the daughter of the house, reared a family and lived until 1860. He is buried in Hardwood cemetery near Kinnegad. Above is a *History of the New Testament* which he owned and on which are written, probably in his own hand, the names of his children, the first, William, being born in 1803.

Appendix 2

List of the Men who Marched with the Wexford Army into Meath in July 1798

Of the thousands, who left Wexford to march with the insurgent army through Wicklow, Kildare and Meath in 1798, little detail is known. As with all armies in history, it was made up of many individuals who were largely anonymous figures, the details of whose lives and deaths are now lost to us forever. In this case, however, we do know details of some of these individuals, extracted from a number of sources. The following are those whose names have been found amongst the records and folk memories which remain. While almost all are from Wexford the list is inclusive of all those who marched with the insurgents after they left Whelp Rock, in County Wicklow, on the night of 9 July 1798.

1. Boland. Recorded on the memorial at Clonard as one of those killed in the battle on 1 July 1798.
2. Byrne, Bryan. Aged fifty-seven years. 5ft 6ins tall with black hair. Captured near Slane in July 1798 by Squire Morris. Charged with 'being with the rebel' and recorded as being on the prison ship *Columbine* on 25 September 1798.
3. Byrne, Charles. Captured and brought before a Court Martial in Slane on 18 July 1798 by order of Gen. Meyrick.
4. Byrne, Daniel. Aged twenty-one. 5ft 9ins tall with brown hair. Captured at Navan by the Drumcondra Infantry Corps. Is likely to have been one of two insurgents of the name D. Byrne treated at Navan infirmary by Dr Neligan in late July and early August 1798. On board the *Columbine* on 25 September 1798.
5. Byrne, Darby. Believed to have come from the area of Tinehealy. Aged eighteen. 5ft 8ins tall with brown hair. Likely to have been the other D. Byrne treated

by Dr Neligan at Navan. Captured at Culmullen by Lord Fingal's Cavalry and charged with rebellion. On the *Columbine* on 25 September 1798.

6. Byrne, Garrett. A descendant of the leadership of great Byrne clan of County Wicklow, Garrett Byrne of Ballymanus was one of the principle leaders of the 1798 insurrection. A brother of Billy Byrne, hanged in Wicklow town, Garrett was named amongst the leadership group at Whelp Rock camp early in July and was probably looked upon as the natural leader of the Wicklowmen. Though he certainly was a major force in the decision making at that time, he is not mentioned after the Battle of Clonard and almost certainly marched back to Glenmalure, with most of the Wicklow contingent, from Carbury Hill on July 12th. He surrendered to Gen. Sir John Moore on 14 July.

7. Byrne, G. Amongst prisoners treated by Dr Neligan on 15 July 1798.

8. Byrne, Hugh. Brother of Miles Byrne of Monaseed who mentions in his memoirs, 'among the brave fellows who escaped and arrived from the Boyne was my poor brother Hugh.'

9. Byrne, John. Uncle of the rebel leader Miles Byrne of Monaseed killed near Ardee. According to Miles' memoirs, 'after they had passed the Boyne at Duleek and near the town of Ardee, where my poor uncle John Byrne was killed in a charge of cavalry by my brother Hugh's side.'

10. Byrne, John. Aged twenty-one. 5ft 10ins tall with black hair. Believed from the area of Tinehealy. Captured by Lord Fingal's Cavalry at Culmullen. On the *Columbine* in September 1798.

11. Byrne, Matthew. Aged twenty-nine. 5ft 6ins tall with black hair. Captured by the County Meath Yeoman Cavalry. Charged with rebellion. On the *Columbine* in September 1798.

12. Byrne, Michael. Before a Court Martial at Slane on 18 July 1798 charged with 'waging war against our Sovereign Lord the King and his Leige Subjects'.

13. Byrne, Patrick. Before a Court Martial at Slane on 18 July 1798.

14. Buckley. By tradition one of the Wexford 'croppies' buried at Lobinstown was of that name.

15. Bush, M. 'Rebel' treated by Dr Neligan on 14 July for 'gunshot wound to the hip'.

16. Callaghan, John. Aged thirty-three. 5ft 3ins tall with brown hair. Gave himself up to the Carlow Militia at Navan. On the *Columbine* in September 1798.

17. Carney, Philip. Charged with rebellion at the Court Martial in Slane on 18 July 1798.

18. Cartan, William. Farmer from Ballyclough. Amongst a group of rebel prisoners recommended for protection by Lord Fingal in 1799.

19. Casey, Murthe. Aged forty-six. 5ft 2ins tall with black hair. Captured by Nobber Cavalry near Navan and treated by D. Neligan for 'gunshot wound of the breast'. On the *Columbine* in September 1798.

20. Cavanagh, Anthony. Charged with rebellion at a Court Martial in Slane on 18 July 1798.

21. Cavanagh. Hid in a large bog near Ardee and survived the hue and cry. Eventually settled down in the area and married a local girl named Farrelly and lived in Rathmore. His Cavanagh descendents are still in the area.

22. Coffey, (John?). Hid in the area of Ardee after the Battle of Knightstown. Was believed to be a schoolmaster from some part of County Wexford. Eventually found work with local farmers, after the area had quietened down, and married and lived at Greenhills, Newtown, Ardee. He had two children, John and Peg. All are buried in Syddan cemetery.

23. Colfer. The Swift family sheltered two Wexfordmen after the Battle of Ballyboughill in north county Dublin. One of them was named Colfer.

24. Connor. P. Rebel prisoner treated for fever by Dr Neligan on 7 August 1798.

25. Coogan. Also called himself Hogan and Edward O'Neill. Wexfordman wounded at Ballyboughill and, 'headed a party of robbers and was endevouring to disturb the neighbourhood'. Captured at a house at the Bog of the Ring, in north County Dublin, by a party led by Henry Baker in late October 1798.

26. Conway. J. Rebel treated for contusion of the shoulder by Dr Neligan on 10 August 1798.

27. Crawley. Shot by Yeomanry at Tankardstown, he managed to survive and to stagger to the house owned by the O'Connells. He asked for a drink of water and told them he was from Wexford and that his name was Crawley. He died of his wounds and is buried in a field at Creewood.

28. D'Arcy, James. Farmer from Monclane. Rebel prisoner recommended for protection by Lord Fingal in 1799.

29. Dempsey, C. Rebel prisoner treated for fever by Dr Neligan on 18 August 1798.

30. Dempsey. Mentioned by Brian Cleary in *The Battle of Oulart Hill* as having returned from the Meath expedition.

31. Dillon, Thomas. Aged twenty-two. 5ft 6ins tall with red hair. Captured in County Meath by Lord Fingal's cavalry. On the *Columbine* in September 1798.

32. Dixon, Thomas. A publican from Castlebridge and one of the principle leaders of the Wexford insurgents. His wife may have travelled with him into Meath as she is mentioned by Holt as having been in north Wicklow on 27 June. He was last reported as having been in Dunboyne on 12 July. What subsequently happened to him is a mystery.

33. Dogherty, Thomas. Charged with rebellion at a Court Martial in Slane on 18 July 1798.

34. Doherty, P. Rebel prisoner treated by Dr Neligan on 6 August 1798.

35. Doorly, John. Kildare man who fought with the Wexford army at Clonard. Captured and hanged at Mullingar.

36. Doran. One of the sixteen Wexfordmen named on the mass grave of those killed at Clonard.

37. Dowd. One of those named on the mass grave of those Wexfordmen killed at Clonard.

38. Doyle, One of those named on the grave at Clonard.

39. Doyle, B. Rebel prisoner treated by Dr Neligan at Navan on 5 August 1798.

40. Doyle, D. Prisoner treated for fever by Dr Neligan in Navan on 3 August 1798.

41. Doyle, Jim. Born in Wexford in 1781 Jim hid for two days in a potato field after the Battle of Clonard. He was eventually taken in by the Whytes of Aughamore and worked for them for a time before marrying a daughter of the house. He was always known in the area as 'The Croppy' and proved an excellent farmer, introducing beekeeping to the area. He died around 1860 and is buried in Hardwood cemetary near Kinnegad. A number of his descendants live in the area.

42. Doyle, Joe. One of the Wexfordmen mentioned by Brian Cleary in *The Battle of Oulart Hill* as having returned safely from Meath.

43. Doyle. According to an account by 'A Contemporary', recalled in 1829, in making their escape after the battle at Knightstown, the decision was made, 'however painful – to dismount the extra horsemen and trust the issue to fortune and their own unsubdued courage.' The account goes on, 'the dismounted men were placed under the trustworthy leadership of a bold and experienced Shelmalier marksman named Doyle who commenced the retreat in orderly and well organised movement.' It is likely that this is the group of forty-eight which crossed the Boyne, at Beaupark, on the night of 15 July and set out for home.

44. Doyne, Daniel. From 'near Gorey' a prisoner who made a statement regarding the events.

45. Duffy, Francis. Aged thirty years. 5ft 10ins with brown hair. Captured at Castlejordan, County Meath, by the Kinnegad Yoemanry. On the *Columbine* in September 1798.

46. Early, John. Aged twenty-three years. 5ft 8ins tall with dark hair. Taken into custody by a Mr Wolfe in County Meath. Treated, as a prisoner for 'gunshot wound to the neck' by Dr Neligan. On the prison ship *Columbine* on 25 September 1798.

47. Farrell, Thomas. Charged with rebellion at a Court Martial in Slane on 18 July 1798.

48. Farrell, Willie. Referred to as Capt. Farrell and clearly a middle-rank leader. He rode into the yard of Tyrrell's house at Clonard and was killed with the first shot in the battle there, by seventeen year old Thomas Tyrrell, firing from an upper window. The gun used by Tyrrell is still extant.

49. Feeley, Michael (see Feeley Joe/Willie).

50. Feeley, Lohey (see Feeley Joe/Willie).

51. Feeley, Joe/Willie. Three Wexford brothers by the name of Feeley, who marched with the rebels, stayed and settled in Meath after 1798. Michael lived at Harlinstown, Lohey at Mullaghmore, in Rathkenny, and Joe (or Willie) lived at Donaghmore, near Navan. They were all tall men who came from somewhere near the Wexford/Carlow border and were all wood turners and carpenters. They made butter dishes, chairs, forms and other household articles for the people of the area.

52. Finn, Laurence. Mentioned by Miles Byrne in his Memoirs.

53. Finn, Luke. Brother to Laurence. In Miles Byrne's *Memoirs* he writes, when telling of a battle near Ardee (possibly Knightstown), how his brother Hugh Byrne

recalled, 'the extraordinary bravery displayed on the same occasion by the two Finns, Laurence and Luke: the latter, being knocked down in the charge and ridden over and trampled down by all the cavalry, kept his musket notwithstanding close by his side – sat up and took deliberate aim.'

54. Finlan, P. (Fenelon?) Prisoner treated by Dr Neligan in Navan in August 1798.

55. Fitzgerald, Edward. One of the principle leaders of the rebellion and probably considered the overall leader of the group which marched to Wicklow. Did not agree with the decision, taken at Whelp Rock, to march into Kildare and Meath, after which the leadership was then assumed by Kearns and Perry. May not have stayed with the march beyond Timahoe on 10 July, and certainly did not remain with the group after Clonard on 11 July. Was one of the signitories of terms of surrender at Rathcoffey House, together with Aylmer and the other Kildare leaders, on 15 July, and surrendered himself to Gen. Dundas at Straffan on 21 July 1798.

56. Flynn, John. Charged at Slane with rebellion on 18 July 1798.

57. Fogarty, Daniel. Aged fifty-five years. 5ft 2ins with black hair. Taken by the Navan Cavalry at Navan and charged with rebellion. Treated, as a prisoner, by Dr Neligan and on the prison ship *Columbine* in September 1798.

58. Fortune, P. Treated, as a prisoner, by Dr Neligan for fever on 5 August 1798.

59. Hanlen, Matthew. Aged 23 years. 5 ft 6ins tall with red hair. Taken prisoner in county Meath by Lord Fingal. On the *Columbine* in September 1798.

60. Hanlen, Daniel. Aged twenty-nine. 5ft 4ins tall with black hair. Taken prisoner near Slane by Yeoman Cavalry. Charged with rebellion at a Court Martial in Slane on 18 July. On the prison ship *Columbine* on 25 September 1798.

61. Hackett. Three or, possibly, four brothers named Hackett marched to Meath and one was killed at the battle of 'the bridge' between Rathkenny and Wilkenstown. The others survived and got safely home to Wexford. One, Joe, returned to Meath.

62. Hackett, Joe. Got safely back to Wexford but returned to Meath a year later and married, it was said, a girl who helped him when he was hiding out in the area. He lived out his life in Wilkenstown. One account given by Michael Biggy of Knock, says, 'My grandfather and old Joe Bradley knew him well. He wore a great big long flowing beard and used to walk down by Knock crossroads when going to the Killary River to fish. He lived to be a very old man.'

63. Harpur. One of those named as having died at the Battle of Clonard and listed on the memorial there.

64. Hoare, Peter. In the days immediately following the battle at Knightstown many Wexford rebels, who were captured in the surrounding districts, were brought to Chamberstown Hill for summary execution. An account by A. Contemporary, recalled in 1829, mentions the evidence of Fr Mulligan. The Revd Mr Mulligan was the priest in Rathkenny in 1798, and he bravely hurried to Chamberstown Hill, probably to plead for leniency and to offer spiritual assistance to the rebels about to be killed. There he was jeered at and, 'encountered every species of rude and repulsive treatment.' Fr Mulligan recalled seeing how the Wexford

prisoners waited, 'the calm composure of some, the lighter carriage of others, but the fortitude and firmness of all.' Having seen the treatment meted out to the priest, one of those about to mount the scaffold shouted, 'Don't mind him your reverence he's only a yeomanry!' He took out a small prayer book and held it open in his hand and said, 'This is for any of you who can read and has the charity to pray for the soul of a Wexfordman.'

The account tells us that the prayer book was subsequently given to a 'pious inhabitant' in the adjoining parish of Castletown where the writer says that he saw it himself, 'It was a double manual; on the title page was written in a fair and legible hand, "Peter Hoare" and on the unprinted leaf to the left was recorded the date of his marriage, and the birth of two of his children.'

65. Hogan. Mentioned as having been killed at Clonard on the memorial there.
66. Holt, Joseph. One of the great Wicklow leaders of 1798. He was one of those who argued vehemently against marching into Kildare and Meath. He returned to Wicklow from Carbury Hill on 12 July. Transported to Australia.
67. Hopkins, John. Aged twenty-two years. 5ft 8ins tall with dark hair. Taken at Navan by Yeoman Cavalry. On the *Columbine* in September 1798.
68. Hopkins, G. Treated, as a prisoner, for fever by Dr Neligan on 13 August 1798.
69. Hore. One of those named on the memorial in Clonard as having been killed at the battle there on 11 July 1798.
70. Kavanagh, B. Treated as a prisoner by Dr Neligan.
71. Kavanagh, M. Treated as a prisoner for six gunshot wounds to the back by Dr Neligan.
72. Kearns, Fr Mogue. Principle promoter of the plan to move into the midlands from the Wicklow Mountains and undisputed leader from Timahoe onwards. Left the Wexford army after the battle at Knightstown and, together with Perry, excaped south to County Offaly. Captured at Wheelabout, Clonbullogue, by a group of Yeomanry lead by Ridgeway on the morning of 18 July. Hanged at Edenderry on 21 July and buried at nearby Monasteroris.
73. Kearns, Roger. From Ballycrystal, Bunclody. First cousin of Fr Mogue. Killed near Ardee (Probably Knightstown).
74. Kearns, Stephen. Brother of Roger from Ballycrystal, Bunclody. Also killed near Ardee.
75. Kearns, Mogue. First cousin of Fr Mogue Kearns. Wounded near Skerries in north Dublin.
76. Kelly, John. One of a group of Wexfordmen escaping from Knightstown and attacked by cavalry at Girley. Kelly escaped and hid in the Clonmellon area until he eventually found employment as a farm labourer. Never married and lived out his life in Archerstown where he is buried and his grave is marked by a memorial.
77. Kelly, G. Prisoner treated by Dr Neligan in July 1798.

78. Kiernan. One of those listed on the memorial as having died at the Battle of Clonard.

79. Kinsella. One of those who returned safely to Wexford, according to Brian Cleary in *The Battle of Oulart Hill*.

80. Kirwan, Peter. One of those charged with rebellion at a Court Martial in Slane on 18 July 1798.

81. Kyan, Esmonde. The last leader in the field with the Wexford insurgents, Kyne was in command at the last battle in Ballyboughill, Co. Dublin, on 14 July 1798. He made good his escape and reached Hugh Harney's cottage, in Glenmalure, over the following days. He could not be persuaded to remain there but headed back to Wexford town where he was captured and hanged.

82. Lacey, Hugh. Aged twenty-two years. 5ft 3ins with brown hair. Reported as being 'a little deaf'. Captured at Kingscourt, County Cavan, by the Lower Kells Cavalry and charged with being with the rebels. Treated by Dr Neligan on 22 July 1798.

83. Lacy, James. Aged twenty-two years. 5ft 5ins tall with brown hair. Captured at Culmullen by Lord Fingal's Cavalry and charged with rebellion.

84. Logan, Thomas. The youngest rebel recorded. Aged fifteen years. 5ft tall with dark hair. Taken by the Lower Kells Cavalry near Navan.

85. Lord, William. Aged thirty-five. 5ft 4ins with black hair. Taken into custody in County Meath shot through the cheek. Treated by Dr Neligan.

86. Madden, Hugh. Aged twenty-five. 5ft 4ins tall with brown hair. Captured, at Tankerstown, by Yeoman Cavalry. Charged with being with the rebels. On the *Columbine* in September 1798.

87. Magrane, Thomas. Charged at a Court Martial in Slane on 18 July 1798, with 'Waging war against our Soverign Lord the King'.

88. Maileia, Thomas. Aged twenty-six. 5ft 7ins tall with dark hair. Taken prisoner at Dunshaughlin.

89. McCann. Gen. Myers mentions McCann as being one of the leaders of the Wexfordmen in Meath (could he have meant Kyan?).

90. McCrath. One of the rebels killed at Clonard whose name is on the memorial there.

91. McDaniel, Patrick. Aged thirty-three. 5ft 3ins. 'Very bad with a rupture. Gave himself up near Dunshaughlin to Lord Fingal's Cavalry. Being with the rebels.'

92. McDonnell, L. Rebel in custody treated by Dr Neligan.

93. McDonnell, M. Prisoner treated by Dr Neligan.

94. McEvoy. Was sheltered by the Smyths of Brownestown when pursued by the militia. Eventually married and settled in Rathbran Mor. Many of his descendents are still in the area.

95. Monahan, Peter. Aged sixteen years. 5ft 5ins with brown hair. Captured by Lord Fingal's Cavalry.

96. Mooney, P. Rebel prisoner treated at Navan by Dr Neligan.

97. Murphy. On the memorial of those killed at Clonard.

98. Murphy. Two mysterious Murphys mentioned. Fr Murphy on a report from Dunboyne and a Fr Thomas Murphy killed at Drakestown Bridge on 14 July. The first may have been named in error though the amount of contemporary evidence for the Drakestown incident is strong and persuasive.

99. Murphy, Joseph. Aged twenty-one. 5ft 5ins with black hair. Captured by Lord Fingal's cavalry.

100. Murphy or Murtagh. In his account Thomas Hickey of Ladyrath recorded that, 'a croppy was kept here by my great-grandfather for over two years. I cannot remember exactly what his name was, but it was either Murtagh or Murphy. He was the heart's blood of a rebel. He was from Gorey.'

101. Murphy, Nicholas. Farmer and shopkeeper from Monaseed. According to Miles Byrne, 'Escaped from the Boyne and got into Dublin, where he was hiding as well as hundreds of our comrades'.

102. Murphy, T. Prisoner treated in July 1798 by Dr Neligan for, 'Fractures of the skull and 23 other wounds'.

103. Murray, Patrick. Aged forty-four. 5ft 6ins with black hair. Gave himself up in Navan to the Navan Cavalry. Being with the rebels. On the *Columbine* in September 1798.

104. Murray, Laurence. Aged eighteen years. 5ft 5ins tall with brown hair. Taken at Rofoy (Rathfeigh) by the Buckingham Militia. Being with the rebels.

105. Murray, Stephen. From near Gorey. A prisoner who gave evidence of events.

106. Mythen. One of those who returned safely to Wexford according to Brian Cleary *Battle of Oulart Hill*.

107. Nolan. One of those listed as having died at the Battle of Clonard.

108. Nowlan, G. Treated for gunshot wound of the shoulder by Dr Neligan in Navan.

(O'Neill Edward see Coogan)

109. O'Neill, Michael. Charged with rebellion at Slane on 18 July 1798.

110. Perry, Anthony. One of the principle leaders. Stayed with Kearns after the Battle of Knightstown and was captured, with him, on 18 July. Executed in Edenderry on 21 July 1798.

111. Purcell, J. Treated as a rebel prisoner for fever on 26 July 1798.

112. Purcell, T. Treated, as a prisoner, for wound of the head.

113. Redmond. Listed on the memorial amongst those killed at Clonard.

114. Redmond, Denis. House carpenter from Kilcavan. With Nicholas Murphy group which escaped to Dublin. Given protection in 1799.

115. Redmond, John Junior. From Kilcavan. Escaped with a group of five to Dublin.

116. Reidy. W. Wexford prisoner treated by Dr Neligan in 1798.

117. Reilly. Named as amongst those killed at Clonard.

118. Reilly, E. Treated as a prisoner for a gunshot wound of the arm by Dr Neligan.

119. Reilly, Luke. Charged with rebellion at Slane on 18 July 1798. Aged twenty-four years. 5ft 4ins with black hair. Taken prisoner by Lord Fingal's cavalry. On the prison ship *Columbine* in September 1798.
120. Reilly, William. Treated at Navan on 6 August 1798, for gunshot wound of the leg, while a prisoner.
121. Roach. Named on the Clonard memorial as one of those killed there on 11 July 1798.
122. Roche, Edward. One of the principle leaders. Would have allied himself with Fitzgerald in his opposition to moving the army from Whelp Rock into Kildare. His involvement afterwards is not clear or is it certain how long he remained with the rebel group. Surrendered to Gen. Hunter, on terms of transportation, in August 1798. Died in Newgate Prison.
123. Rochford. One of those listed as having died at Clonard.
124. Rowe. An account by Joseph Everard (b. 1879) of Rathdrinagh tells of a Wexford rebel shot in the shoulder by a yeoman commanded by Maj. Gorge. He excaped and was hidden by the Madden family until his wound healed and he left for home. He says, 'His name was Rowe and he was a Protestant'.
125. Ryan. One of those who returned safely to Wexford according to Brian Cleary in *The Battle of Oulart Hill*.
126. Shanon. Patrick. Aged twenty-four. 5ft 2ins with black hair. Gave himself up in Navan. Charged with rebellion.
127. Sheron, P. Treated, as a prisoner, for contusion of the breast, by Dr Neligan.
128. Sinnott. One of those named on the memorial as having died in the battle at Clonard.
129. Tongue, James. Charged with rebellion at a Court Martial in Slane on 18 July 1798.
130. Walsh. Hidden by Watsons, of Springhill in north County Dublin, after the battle at Ballyboughill. His son became a priest and visited the Watsons some forty years later.
131. Whelan, Timothy. From, Askasilla, Blackwater. In an account of the Battle of Knightstown, Whelan is specifically mentioned and would appear to have been a middle rank leader.

Appendix 3

Troops amd Militia in Action Against the Wexfordmen in County Meath

The Cavalry and Infantry of Drogheda garrison. Commanded by Gen. Weymes.

The Navan Cavalry garrison. Commanded by Brig.-Gen. Meyrick.

Carlow Militia, Navan.

The City of Limerick Regiment (Rathangan). Commanded by Col. Vereker.

County Limerick Militia (Edenderry). Commanded by Col. Gough. Also Maj. Ormsby, Lt Coys and Lt Grace.

Dumfries Light Dragoons. Commanded by Col. Maxwell. Also Capt. Arch Gordon and Capt. Douglas.

Royal Buckinghamshire Militia.

Duke of York's Royal Inverness Highlanders. Commanded by Maj.-Gen. Alex Campbell. Also Col. J. Gordon.

Durham Cavalry. Commanded by Lt Col. Orde.

Fermanagh Militia. Commanded by Lt Lucas and Lt Gabot.

Northumberland Highlanders.

Northumberland Fencibles.

7th Dragoon Guards.

Mullingar Garrison. Commanded by Col. Blake.

Lower Kells Cavalry (Yeomanry).

Kinnegad Yeomanry.

Lord Fingal's Cavalry (Yeomanry).

County Meath Yeoman Cavalry.

Drumcondra Infantry Corps (Yeomanry)

Nobber Cavalry (Yeomanry).

Navan Cavalry (Yeomanry).

Tankerstown Yeoman Cavalry.

Balbriggan Cavalry (Yeomanry).

Trim 8th Cavalry (Yeomanry).

Trim Yeoman Infantry.

Rathcore Rangers (Yeomanry).

Carton Militia (Yeomanry).

Coolock Cavalry (Yeomanry). Commanded by Sir Henry Wilkinton.

Swords Infantry (Yeomanry).

Lord Gormanstown's Corps (Yeomanry).

Kilbrew Yeoman Cavalry. Commanded by Capt. Gorges.

Ballyna Cavalry (Yeomanry).

Clonard Corps (Yeomanry).

Kinnegad Cavalry (Yeomanry). Commanded by Lt Haughton and Lt Coppertwaite.

Edenderry Cavalry (Yeomanry). Commanded by Capt. Ridgeway.

Capt. Wahely's troop of Yeomanry.

Yeomanry Corps of Dublin.

Cooleystown Cavalry (Yeomanry).

Warrenstown Cavalry (Yeomanry).

Gen. Myers, Gen. Dundas and Capt. Barry were also involved, in what command I cannot ascertain. The above list may not be complete.

Appendix 4

Contemporary Correspondence

All of the surviving contemporary letters are those written by soldiers and officials on the Government side, the only rebel versions being those recollected and recorded much later. While these documents are important, due account must be taken of the rather one-sided and predictable perspective of those opposing the insurgents, when reviewing the events.

Letter from Lt-Col. Gough to Col. Verecher.
Edenderry, 12 July 1798.

My Dear Col.,

Yesterday evening I received a letter at Philipstown from Major Ormsby saying that he had very good reason to think this town would be attacked last night by the rebels. I immediately came here with a Detachment to his assistance. At eight o'clock this morning I heard that they were in great force at Carbury Hill. I instantly marched out with the Co. Limk. City Militia, 207 Dragoon Guards and 10 Yeomen of Captain Wakeley's Troop. On my arrival there I found that they had moved on at daylight to Johnstown after destroying everything at Lord Herberton's house. Their march was easily traced as they left all the country in flames as they passed, and on my arrival at Johnstown I found it entirely consumed. There I learned they were not far ahead, but in immense force.

In less than half an hour I came in sight of them, strongly posted on the Hill of Knockderig (Rynville), drawn up and forming such a line as really astonished me, with many standards flying and everything prepared to give me battle.

My little detachment attacking such a multitude I saw as a desperate undertaking. But following them for 12 miles, being witness to their horrid conduct that morning in their march, and knowing the justice of my cause, made me determine immediately to attack them at all events.

On my halting to arrange my mode of attack, they thought I would and yelled most horribly. I then posted C Miller and the 207 D.G. on a road leading to their right with orders, if possible to charge them the moment he saw them give way. And I marched nearer to their left as that part of the hill was easiest of access for infantry. I found the column under cover of a strong ditch. They soon began firing on me from some corn fields and from behind ditches in their front. And their main body commenced firing as soon as I came within their reach.

I saw I had nothing to save us but a desperate attack. I moved in briskly and formed up when within one field of the main body, and fired as fast as we could, advancing. In some minutes I saw they began to get in confusion. I then quickened my pace and fire and they soon fled in every direction covering many large fields. Unfortunately the closeness of the country prevented the cavalry pursuing or the slaughter must have been immense.

I took and brought here from their camp 161 fat bullocks and cows, 53 horses, 7000 yards of new linen, besides numberless small things the men could carry. I also destroyed 40 sheep and 3 bullocks they had just killed and were preparing for dinner, three hogsheads of whiskey, some port wine, 18 sacks of flour, 3 bags of G powder, 1 bag of slugs, a quantity of lead, a car of groceries and a swivel they had not time to mount. I also left many horses in the field so wounded they could not travel. To have waited to bring them all off would take much time, and had they rallied we might be cut off before we could get home as they had near 4000 men.

Nothing ever exceeded the spirited and gallant manner by which the officers and soldiers attacked them. I cannot find words adequate to their merit to thank them. To Major Ormsby I am particularly indebted.

The rebels had near 150 killed and wounded dispersed among the corn fields and ditches where we drove them. I have had but two Limk. M. killed and five wounded.

Major Ormsby, Lieut. C. Grace of the Lim.M., Lieut Cartland of the Yeoman Cavalry, and Com. Millar of the Drag.G. were the officers of my detachment. The Hon. Geo. Brown came with me as a volunteer, to whom I am exceedingly indebted. He was forward on all occasions, and on seeing a rebel officer shot, gallantly galloped up and took a large, handsome green standard which we have brought home.

I hear they retreated to near Trim, and were that day commanded by Col. Aylmer, Capt. Dooley, Kerns, a priest, Capt. Scoby and Fitzgerald. This country is in a wretched situation.

I am, my dear Col. Yours very sincerely,
G. Gough, Lt. Col. L.C.M.
Colonel Verecher,
Limk. City Regt., Rathangan.

(National Archives 620/436/1)

Official Dispatch to the Duke of Portland.
Dublin Castle, 15 *July* 1798.

My Lord,

I have the honour to acquaint your Grace that it being reported that the mountains of Wicklow were receptacle for bodies of rebel fugitives, I directed Lieut.-General Lake to move different columns in various directions to clear that part of the country. He returned to-day to Dublin and reports that he was not able to find any body whatever assembled in any part of the district. The Lieut.-General gives the highest credit to the perseverance and spirit of the troops during very long and difficult marches through a country almost inaccessible for troops.

On Monday last [9 July] those rebels who had been in the mountains passed over to the Bog of Allen. On Wednesday they attacked with a body of about 1,500 the town of Clonard, where they were repulsed with a loss of 60 men by Colonel Blake, who marched from Mullingar with about 50 infantry and as many Yeoman Cavalry to attack them.

This body of Rebels, after their defeat, proceeded towards Kilcock and were pursued till night by a Detachment under Brigadier-Gen. Meyrick.

The Rebel Army advanced to Dunboyne, and on Friday moved to Garristown Hill, whither I ordered Major-General Myers with a Detachment of Royal Bucks Militia and Yeomanry from the Garrison of Dublin to pursue them. The Rebels, however, went for the Boyne and passed it, but were checked near Stackallen by Cavalry detached from two Columns commanded by Major-General Wemys and Brigadier-General Meyrick, who had assembled on the road to Slane. And I have the honour to transmit to your Grace a copy of a letter received by my Military Secretary, Captain Taylor, from Major-General Wemys giving an account of the action.

I have the further satisfaction to acquaint your Grace that last night about 7 o'clock Capt. Gordon of the Dumfries Fencibles with a Detachment of Infantry and Cavalry, fell in with that part of the Rebels which had returned across the Boyne near Garristown, killed 20 of them and took 200 horses.

I have the honor to be, my Lord,

Your Grace's most obedient and humble servant.

(National Archives 620/39 -80)

Letter from Maj.-Gen. Wemys to Capt. Taylor.
Drogheda, 15*th July* 1798.

Sir,

Having received information from different quarters on Friday afternoon, that a large body of Rebels had assembled about Garristown and were marching towards this, I went out with what force I thought prudent to take from Garristown here to Duleek, where I arrived at ten o'clock at night, the 13th, and I got information that the rebels were strongly posted upon a hill 3 miles off to the right.

Not knowing the country, I remained in Duleek till one o'clock when I marched to the hill. I found the rebels left it at our coming into Duleek the evening before, and halted at a village near it. I followed them to the village. They had left it about 5 hours before towards Slane.

I thought it probable from a note I had received from General Meyrick that he was to march from Tara Hill to attack the rebels near Garristown, that I should hear of him at the Black Lion. I went on about half a mile when I saw General Meyrick's Division coming into the Black Lion. We immediately proceeded by two roads towards Slane, as we were informed they were posted above Lord Boyne's House. When we came there, they had left it about three hours and had passed the Boyne above Slane. Finding that we did not come up with them, General Meyrick sent on Lt-Col. Orde with the Durham Cavalry to overtake them and keep them in check, which he did, about five miles on the S. side of the Boyne road to Ardee. He sent back for reinforcements of cavalry. I ordered Col. Maxwell with the Dumfries with General Meyrick to move on, and they found the rebels very strongly posted behind a defile between two bogs, the pass only allowing to form by fours.

The Cavalry were in their advanced post and charged with great spirit, but from the position of the enemy, Col. Maxwell thought it better to wait till the infantry came up, which it did with the Northumberland Highlanders in a very short time, and advanced with my Battalion guns. Whenever the rebels perceived this, I saw them get into confusion, and they immediately broke in all directions. I then ordered the Cavalry and Yeomanry to attack, and I followed with the Infantry to support them. But the rebels got into the Bogs and the Cavalry advanced, killed all they met with, and surrounded the Bog to the height on the opposite side. The Highlanders got into the Bog and killed all that were in it. Those who got out on the opposite side were met with the Cavalry.

From the manner in which they dispersed, I cannot give an exact account of the killed. We took a great quantity of pikes, pistols, swords, muskets, etc., and two standards. General Meyrick got one prisoner, who gave him some information, and promised him more. He took him with him to Navan, so that I cannot report anything with accuracy about him.

The troops behaved with great spirit and bore a great deal of fatigue, particularly General Meyrick's Division, with a reinforcement from this of the Dumfries, and my Light Company had been out three nights. I am particularly indebted to the Gentlemen Yeomanry, and to Mr. Trotter, Duleek, who served me as a guide. Any body of the Rebels left went on towards Ardee, a great many got round the hill on our right, and came back to Slane, where they assembled near it, and passed the Boyne and went back towards Garristown, where I hope General Myers would fall in with them.

I reported this to General Campbell last night operating under his command. I just now received a note from him to inform you of it.

I have the honor to be, Sir, your most obetd.,

Weymes M. G., Northuml. Highlanders.

(National Archives 620/39/85)

Letter from Col. J. Gordon to Lord Castlereagh.
Trim, 15th July 1798.

My Lord,

I have the honour, etc. The day before yesterday I pursued the Rebels from about Longwood to Kulmullen when the night came on and no account could be got of them than that they dispersed in all directions. We killed about thirty of their detached parties and stragglers, and returned here after a march of 14 hours without halt.

I have the honor also to inform your Lordship that a Detachment of my Regt. came up yesterday with a party of Rebels consisting of sixteen with as many horses. The Rebels fired on my detachment without effect, who attacked them and killed fifteen and brought one prisoner in – a very young boy who was the servant of Capt. Knox Grogan, who was killed in Wicklow. The boy is most intelligent, and I expect to have the honor of sending some useful information to your Lordship tomorrow.

I have the honor to be, my Lord
Your Lordship's most obed. and faithful, humble servt.,
J. Gordon, Colonel.
Duke of York's,
Royal Regt. of Highlanders.

(National Archives 620/39/86)

Letter from Capt. Arch Gordon to Lord Castlerea.

My Lord,

I think it necessary to acquaint your Lordship that having recd information this morning about 8 o'clock of the Mail Coach having been attacked and carried off from Corduff, I proceeded with a party from the Dumfries Fen. Cavalry & Balbriggan Cavalry to Robertstown, where I recd information of the coach having been conveyed, and where we were told a considerable number of robbers were collected.

On our arrival there, we found the Mail Coach and that they had proceeded to Garristown to which place we instantly pushed on. Within about half a mile of it, we came up with an armed party of Rebels, ten of whom were killed on the road & in ditches. At the time we observed large parties of Cavalry forming on the Hill of Garristown, which was in front to the number of at least 4 or 500 & also infantry in great numbers, whose number as they lined the hedges was impossible to form an idea of. Our horses being much jaded and from their forming parties, as if they had an intention of surrounding us, from the small number under my command, I did not think myself authorized to proceed further.

We have every reason to think their force will receive considerable addition in the course of the night & I conceive that an effectual attack cannot be made upon them without an addition to the infantry force which is at present in this part of the country. The Rebels appear to have taken their position on the Hill of Garristown which is surrounded on the North and East by a very large bog where Cavalry cannot act nor indeed in any part of the country thereabouts, which is everywhere divided by thick hedges.

I have the honor to be My Lord,
Your most obt Servt,
Arch. Gordon Capt.
Dumfries Dragoons,
Nag's Head. 4 o'clock. (July 12th 1798)

(National Archives 620/4/37)

Letter from Maj.-Gen. Myers to Maj.-Gen. Hewitt.
Somerville, Black Lion. 15th July 1798.

My dear Hewitt,

I received last night your letter and now I have to acquaint you that we arrived here last evening, and near this heard of a body of the Rebels having returned through this about an hour before us, and on our right towards Garristown.

This morning I dispatched 50 Cavalry under Capt. Batty in pursuit of them. He did not come up with them, but they fled so frightened that he found on the road several pikes and took ten tired horses. I learn this morning that Capt. Gordon of the Dumfries Fencibles, who I found yesterday at Curraha and left there, received intelligence of them and pursued them also, and that he overtook them, killed 15, and the remainder dispersed in all directions, which at this season they can the more easily do as they conceal themselves in the standing corn. These men, part of the body I was in pursuit of, which body General Meyrick had overtaken at Nobber and dispersed them with considerable loss. Their number yesterday were about 2,000, to-day they are not to be heard of, except that my Lord Fingal informs me this morning that he heard there is a body of them collecting at Culmullen hills. He has sent out a patrol from Kileen, where he is, and we are ready to move towards them whenever we learn of them.

General Weymes was with Merrick yesterday. He returned to Drogheda and Meyrick to Navan. Their troops as well as mine are very much fatigued. The enemy, the main body of them, are certainly fled towards the North and will probably endeavor to enter the County of Cavan at Kingscourt. They are composed of the Banditti from Wexford, Wicklow, Kildare, and are commanded by Murphy, who has reported to have been killed, Roche McCann and others. None of the people of this part of the Country have joined them, but the vagabonds have robbed and plundered the whole country, and I am persuaded that the lively zeal that has been against them saved the country from total destruction. As it is, the devastation is very great. I shall be glad to hear from you and beg you to acquaint Lord Cornwallis with the purpose of this letter.

I remain, very yours truly,
General Myers.

(National Archives 620/29/83)

Letter from Capt. Arch. Gordon to Lord Castlereagh.

My Lord,

I have the honor of writing your Lordship from the Nag's Head on Friday last (13), mentioning my having fallen in with a considerable body of the Rebels at Garristown, and from the small number of the force with me, I did not think myself authorized to attack them.

Having that evening received a reinforcement of one company of the Fermanagh Militia, part of the Coolock Cavalry, and of the Swords Infantry, I marched from this [Balbriggan] at one o'clock on Saturday [a.m.] with them. Fifty of the Carlow Militia, and part of the troops of the Dumfries Cavalry under my command, and Fingal and Balbriggan Cavalry, and being joined on the road by Lord Gormanstown's Troop, my whole force consisted of 100 cavalry and 130 infantry.

I proceeded towards Garristown in hopes of falling in with the party I had seen the preceding day, but on arriving there, found they had, the evening before, gone from thence towards Slane and Navan; in which direction I thought it advisable to proceed, more particularly as I thought it probable I should fall in with General Myers who, I understand, was to take the route from Dublin.

On arriving at Curraghhaw at 11 o'clock [a.m.] I received instructions from the General [Myers] to wait his coming at that place; and in pursuance of his orders, I had prepared to remain there during the night.

At four o'clock I received information that a large body of Rebels, to the amount of several hundreds, were within half a mile of us, and which I afterwards saw move towards Garristown, I considered it my duty to pursue them with the force under my command and, after having followed them to within a mile of Garristown and from thence towards Ballyboughill, I found it would be impossible, as they were well mounted, to bring the infantry up before dark, as they were then a mile in their rear. I accordingly ordered the Dumfries, Fingal, Balbriggan and Coolock Cavalry to pursue and charge them, which they did with great spirit. I thought it necessary to detain Lord Gormanstown's Corps to act with the infantry as soon as they could get up.

The Rebels, on perceiving the Cavalry advance, dismounted and fled in every direction; and on the arrival of the infantry not more than a hundred remained on the ground, who also dispersed on the first discharge and were pursued and cut down by Lord Gormanstown's troop.

The Cavalry being ordered to charge, pursued with the greatest alacrity for upwards of five miles, and from the number killed by them in the pursuit and by the Infantry when they came up with the main body, I have no doubt that there must have been from 150 to 200 killed, 200 horses were taken, and a few pikes and pistols.

Official report from Navan on the state of the district, dated 15 July 1798, given by H. Johnston, signing as the Constable. In it he states that 400 rebels were killed at Knightstown.

It is with peculiar satisfaction I have to mention that this service was affected without any loss on our part, except one horse of the Dumfrieshire killed.

It is but doing justice to the Carlow and Fermanagh Militia to say that after a very severe march of 18 hours, they pressed forward with the greatest spirit and alacrity. The exertions of the Dumfrieshire and Yeomanry answered my warmest expectations.

I have the honor to be, my Lord,
Your Lordship's most obedt Servt.,
Arch. Gordon, Capt. Dumfries Light Dragoons.
Balbriggan, 15th July.

(National Archives 620/39/87)

Letter from Capt. Batty to Lord Castlerea.

Barracks, Malahide,
15th July, 1798.
My Lord,

Having had the honor of a personal interview with your Lordship last Friday evening at the Mayoralty House, I take the liberty of acquainting you with the particulars of our proceedings afterwards.

I then told your Lordship that a party, consisting of part of the Fermanagh Reg. under the command of Lt. Lucas and Gibbot, a detachment of Swords infantry, under the command of Capt. Gordon of the Swords Infantry, and a party of the Coolock Cavalry under my command, had gone out in the consequence of receiving information that the Rebels had taken the Main Coaches from the North Road that morning, and that we had met with a party of Horse from Balbriggan under the command of Capt. Gordon of the Dumfries Fencibles at a place called the Nag's Head, between Ballyboughill and the Naul, who had fallen in with the Rebels and killed 20 of their advance Guard, but not having any infantry with them, thought it imprudent to advance on them.

The Fermanagh, Swords and Coolocks then determined to halt at the Man of War till reinforced by the remainder of the troops from Swords and Malahide; then to proceed with the Force from Balbriggan to attack the Rebels then at Garristown; and I accordingly undertook taking on an Express to your Lordship, and returned to the Man of War.

On my return I found a reinforcement of the Coolock Cavalry and of the Fermanagh Militia under the command of Lt. Fortescal of the Coolock, waiting for me at Swords. We then passed on, having cars to carry the infantry, to the Man of War; but on our arrival there, found that Capt. Gordon of the Swords Inf., who commanded the party from this, had received orders from Capt Gordon of the Dumfries Fencibles to take his party on to Balbriggan, and after mentioning to Capt. Gordon of the Dumfries the purport of the instructions I received, and remonstrating on what Capt. Gordon of the Swords and the officers of the Fermanagh and Coolock thought of the impropriety of our leaving our own Barracks merely to protect Balbriggan, he consented to take us out towards Garristown.

We left Balbriggan at daylight with a force consisting, as nearly as I could calculate, of one hundred Horse and 100 Foot. With these we marched to Garristown where we were joined by 35 or 40 of the Gormanstown Cavalry. Not meeting with the enemy, we halted at a village called Currahaw, near Mr. Gorge's of Kilbride, where after some time, General Myers with forces under his command passed by and ordered us to halt there till six o'clock this morning, and then to return to our respective quarters if nothing should happen in the meantime.

Capt. Gordon of the Dumfries, who commanded the party at Currahaw, sent an Express about 2 o'clock in the afternoon to Gen. Myers. On the return of the Express, he saw a considerable party of the Rebels about a mile from the place we then lay at, and having narrowly escaped, came in, on which we were immediately ordered under arms, and in a very short time we were out.

There is a considerable bog near Currahaw. It lay on the left, and on the opposite side of the bog we were able to see the Rebels advancing in great force down the Hill of Garristown. We, however, came up with them after a pursuit of about 10 miles, near Ballyboughill, where they formed in a field about 200 yards from the road, where we attacked them. In a short time the Rebels abandoned their horses and ran in all directions. A great number were killed. Those who escaped hid, I presume, in the corn fields as we could not afterwards see them. They hid in the field they formed on, every preparation for remaining, last night we took more than 300 horses that they left behind at their intended camp. Night coming on, and not having any shelter for the troops, who were most harassed, not being able to discover where the enemy had gone we returned to our respective quarters. The Rebels appeared to be very badly armed, and I have just heard that there were a number of them unarmed about the fields near Ballyboughill this morning. Lest we should get any information of their again assembling request your Lordship's directions.

I have the honor to be, my Lord,
Your Lordship's obedt, humble servant,
J. Batty, L.C., Coolock.

Appendix 5

Commemoration

The few days in the month of July in 1798, when the Wexford rebels made their final stand in County Meath and surrounding counties, and the memory of the activity during the weeks which followed, of bodies and burials, searches and executions, captures and trials, left an enduring mark on the people of the whole area. As time passed into years the stories of these young men, who had arrived unexpectedly to fight and die, to be captured and transported or, with luck, survive and return to their homes, became deeply embedded in the folk memory of every parish. For the people of the time, and the generations of their descendents to the present day, it is a credit to their generosity of spirit that they they took these young patriots to their hearts and were kind to their memory.

Meath strongly supported the cause of the United Irishmen and very many Meathmen had bravely fought and died in the early days of the rebellion. This may go some way to explaining the care with which the burial places of insurgent Wexfordmen, who had died in the fields of Meath, were marked and remembered throughout the county. In most cases people marked the graves by placing large stones on the headland or roadside and, in order to make clear their significance, it was the practice to whitewash these stones whenever those living nearby were using the wash for their houses. In other cases the old Irish tradition of building a cairn on the site became the practice. In an account, given by Patrick Doggett in 1938, he told us, 'There is a croppies grave at Crock-an-Awr and there used to be a heap of stones beside it. As people passed by each would throw a pebble on it.' In another account of a grave near Collon, Nicholas Weldon, who was born in 1886, recalled this grave covered over by a medium sized heap of stones, 'My father used to tell me to throw a stone on this grave whenever he knew I was to pass that way.'

In later years more formal memorials were raised to mark the battles and gravesites. In the centenary year of 1898 a commemoration committee was formed to promote this work and fifty years later, in 1948, further tribute was paid to the memory of those times.

In 1998, the events of 1798 were celebrated widely throughout County Meath, as well as in north county Dublin and in Kildare, Cavan and Offaly. The involvement of the Wexford rebels, in Meath in particular, was central to many of the ceremonies which were attended by large crowds of people, including ranks of pikemen groups. These modern pikemen, organised by Bill Murray of Templenacroha, County Wexford, who were to be seen at centres from Edenderry to Mountainstown, added greatly to the many dignified and moving ceremonies, bringing a sense of reality to the history of those times.

In Meath, and elsewhere, many new memorials were erected at important locations and many of the grave sites of the young 'croppies' were properly marked and recorded. A number of committees were formed for the purpose and the results of their commitment and determination are now to be seen throughout the area, bringing honour to those whose generosity and pride moved them to undertake these worthy projects.

The North Meath Committee, under the chairmanship of Noel Curtis of Creewood with dedicated members Seamus Kearns, Jim Kearns and Johnny Cassidy erected a fine stone memorial at Horistown, Rathkenny, and placed white steel crosses at five other sites:

Above is a copy of a centenary certificate issued to Thomas McGrath in 1898. Thomas lived until the 1950s and the certificate was discovered in the ruins of his house about 1990. The counter signature is that of James Gammons, who owned the public house in Lobinstown at that time.

Wexford pikemen marching at the site of the impressive memorial erected in Mountainstown in 1998.

1. Creewood. At the grave in Wall's field beside the river.
2. Newtown, Grangegeeth. At the grave in Dillon's field beside the river.
3. Miller's Hill. At the roadside. (Local tradition states that a 'croppy' and a Yeoman are both buried here.)
4. Horristown. At a roadside grave.
5. Gernonstown, Rushwee. At a roadside grave.

A map of local grave sites, prepared by Yvonne Curtis, was also placed on the 'famine wall' in the old church.

At nearby Mountainstown the Mountainstown Commemoration Committee, with Diana Pollock to the fore, erected a beautiful and impressive limestone memorial on her lands at Mountainstown. The Pollock family were in this location in 1798 and are remembered for the great compassion and humanity with which they treated the young rebels. The local liberal magistrate was Mr John Pollock, a supporter of Home Rule and Catholic Emancipation, and many remembered him as having given his protection to those rebels found hiding in the district. One account, passed down by Kate Rogers of Cloughree, from 1884, tells us, 'I often heard it said that John Pollock of Mountainstown was very kind to any of the insurgents who were lucky enough to approach him for his help in '98.'

Others very much involved in this project were Diana's daughter-in-law Atalanta Pollock, Oliver Ward, and Revd William Richie.

In addition to existing memorials at which ceremonies were organised, new memorials were unveiled at Rathkenny, Mountainstown, Kells, Onganstown, Fordstown, Kilmessan, Rathfeigh, Ardcath, Duleek, Stamullen, An Foidin, Trim, Culmullen, Ryndville (Knockderrig), Dunshaughlin, Dunboyne, Navan and Curragha in County Meath, at Ballyboughill and Garristown in County Dublin and Mullagh in County Cavan.

Following a public meeting in Culmullen Hall a committee was formed to commemorate the bicentenary of the events in Culmullen and the surrounding area in 1798. Seventeen people undertook the task of fundraising, research, design, site identification and all the onerous and detailed work involved with the acquisition and erection of suitable memorials. The response of the local people in fund raising, and general support for the project, was magnificent and, as a result, the committee succeeded in erecting twenty grave stone memorials, of Wicklow granite, at thirteen locations, as well as a handsome monument at Culmullen.

Individuals such as Paddy Pryle, Noel Curtis, Niall O'Riordan, Oliver Condon, John Cassidy and many many others too numerous to record, gave freely of their time and energy in pursuance of the bicentennial commemoration in their own areas.

Other local groups and historical societies contributed to the effort which resulted in a number of worthy plaques and memorials being erected throughout the county, completing a wonderful and generous effort by the proud and loyal people of County Meath.

The commitment went beyond Meath. In north county Dublin the last stand of the rebels at Ballyboughill was wonderfully marked with marches and gatherings on the important sites. Here Sean Mac Philbin was to the fore in organising the commemoration, the highlight of which was the huge gathering on 12 July for the unveiling of plaques and recollection of the historic events of two hundred years before.

The men of '98 are long gone to their reward but the people of today have done rich honour to their memory. Future generations, seeing their memorials, will be reminded not to forget.

Tom Doyle struck the anvil one clear sounding blow,
We've left but our lives and our honour we know,
Come on lads the time for remembering is past,
And the pikes in our hands which we'll bear till the last.

In the long days to come this old anvil will tell,
With a prayer and a pike and a Shelmalier yell,
Of the last of the Wexfordmen marching to death,
Unblemished, undaunted, true men while they'd breath.

T.D.Sinnott.

References and Notes

(S.P. refers to State Papers (Rebellion Papers) at the National Archives in Bishop Street, Dublin 8)

Chapter 1

1. Pitchcapping was a most cruel and barbaric torture which involved molten tar in a cardboard cone being placed on the head of the unfortunate captive. It was said to have been devised by a member of the North Cork Militia known as 'Tom the Devil', who certainly was a regular practitioner of the torture throughout county Wexford. It was remembered that, long after the rebellion in the 1840s and 1850s, old men who had suffered pitchcapping and whose scalps were deformed as a result, were allowed to wear hats or woollen caps at Sunday Mass, and remain at the back of churches in places such as Kilmuckridge and Curracloe.
2. Kenny's Hall, where the 'big meeting' took place after the capture of Wexford, is sometimes referred to as Cullimore's Inn, and is currently occupied by Penney's Stores. It was said to have been the largest public hall in the town in 1798 and was a building of the Elizabethan period. Cromwell lodged in the same premises during his occupancy of the town in 1649.

Chapter 2

1. Furlong, Nicolas, *Fr John Murphy of Boolavogue*. (Geography Publications).
2. Pearse, Col. Hugh, *Memoirs of the Life and Military Service of Viscount Lake*.

Chapter 3

1. Croker C., *Memoirs of Joseph Holt*.
2. *Life of Michael Dwyer* states that the rebels arrived at Whelp Rock on 5 July, p.. 46-47.
3. S.P. 620/51/48.
4. *Ibid*.
5. Croker C., *Memoirs of Joseph Holt*.
6. *Ibid*.
7. Memoirs of Miles Byrne.
8. Croker C., *Memoirs of Joseph Holt*.
9. S.P. 620/36/4.

Chapter 4

1. MacSuibhne, Peadar, *Kildare in '98*.
2. *Ibid*.
3. *Ibid*.
4. Holt recorded that the insurgent army at Whelp Rock were, 'very deficient in powder and cartridge.'

Chapter 5

1. 'Kinnegad Parish '82'.
2. S.P. 620/36/4.
3. Another account in a narrative of the engagement, published by John Jones of Dublin in 1799 declares that, 'the 27 men fired upwards of 1,300 ball cartridge.'
4. John Robinson of Kilrathmurray says that Garrett Robinson, who walled in the grave of the Wexfordmen in 1883, was evicted from his holding principally as a result of this action.
5. John Robinson also has a tradition, passed on to him by his father that a woman named Roche came to Clonard from Wexford, after the fighting, looking for her son. It was remembered that she travelled in a cart with solid, spokeless, wooden wheels. The wheels were in such bad condition from the journey that they had to be replaced before she could travel back home.
6. John Robinson says that John Doorly had succeeded in crossing the Boyne but stopped and made a number of attempts to fire his gun at his pursuers. Unfortunately his powder had become wet and would not fire, but the delay allowed him to be captured. Such was the haste with which he was brought into Mullingar and hanged, that his clothes were still dripping water as he swung from the rope.

Chapter 6

1. Lord Harberton was not in residence when the house was raided and his servant, Bryan Forde, wrote to him three days later informing him, in detail, of the rebel's visit. In his letter of Saturday, 4 July 1798, he stated that he was, 'heartly sorry to inform your Lordship that, on Wednesday last, from 6 in the evening till five in the morning that this house were full of rebels & upward of a thousand at a camp in Carberry. The same night they have robbed the house of table linen, sheets, blankets and quilts and several other articles too numerous for insertion'. He said that he had thought to write the following day but could not get anyone willing to deliver the letter until Saturday, when he reported that 'The bearer is a small boy of one of the cotties children, no other person would dare go'.

    A petition lodged in 1802 *(537/270)* by Bryan Forde – 'late under agent to the late Lord Harberton, Co. Kildare' for payment of the amount of £68-17-11 for goods lost on the night of 11 July 1798. The claim was for:

    > 5 new shirts at 12s. £9
    > 9 squares of Muslin at 6s 6d. £2 18s 6d
    > 4 Lawn Handkerchiefs at 2s 2d. 8s 8d
    > A new Hat. £1 2s 9d
    > A great coat. £1 15s
    > 2 cassmere vests. £1 3s 1d
    > 1 pair boots. £1 9d
    > 4 pair cotton stockings at 5s 5d. £1 1s 8d
    > 1 pair knee buckles. 6s 6d
    > 2 suits new clothes. £9
    > 1 new saddle. £2 5s 6d
    > 3 pair new shoes. £1 2s 9d
    > Cash by Sheerin an approver. £1 14s 1½d
    > Silver watch with gold seals. £9 13s 4½d
    > Cash paid for taking up robbers and murderers. £7 19s 3d
    > Mare broken down by the rebels and of no use to me. £17 1s 3d
    > £68 17s 11d

    Despite a slight inaccuracy in his addition or, perhaps, an item being overlooked in the account, the claim was paid under Secret Service payments.

2. Knockderrig is a place name which has fallen out of use and, indeed, seems to have been replaced by the time of the Ordnance Survey in the first half of the nineteenth century. It is now known as Rynville, and is a mile or two north of Enfield (which was itself known as New Inn in 1798).

3. In a description of the battle, written on the following day, (*Faulkner's Journal*, 21 July 1798) the writer stated:

> Col. Gough followed the rebels upwards of 12 miles to the hill of Nockderrig within two miles of Johnstown, where they were strongly posted. On Col. Gough's getting sight of the rebels, he immediately drew up his forces & resolved to attack them, though their numbers were above 5,000. He ordered the cavalry, under, command of Cornet Miller of the 7th Dragoon Guards, to take their post on a road leading to the hill & charge the enemy when he had broke them. The Colonel then marched his men up a narrow lane leading to the hill, but finding that he might be annoyed from behind the hedges, he wheeled to the right under cover of a large ditch, which the rebels perceiving gave three cheers & shewed their whole force. Col. Gough then advanced briskly up the hill under heavy fire which had little effect, the enemy's bullets flying over their heads. The Colonel, with much difficulty, prevented his men from firing till they had come within reach of them, when he commenced a steady, well directed, fire which lasted about 20 minutes.

4. I am unable to ascertain the date of the killing of the rebels at Lawlesses Barn (see under graves/Gaulstown), but it would seem likely, given the location, that the men involved were amongst those who dropped out of the main body, during their march from Knockderrig to Dunboyne.

5. There was a strong belief in Meath that a Fr Murphy had led the Wexfordmen and had been killed at Drakestown bridge. (See A Mystery Man of '98 in the appendices.)

6. According to a local account the Government forces, on learning of the approach of the rebel army, placed six pieces of cannon at a strategic point on the Slane to Ardee road, on the hill at Collon cross roads, to prevent their move north.

7. According to an account by Fr McManus.

8. Col. Gordon also reported that, 'my party brought in here all their horses, watches, money &c &c to a considerable amount'.

Chapter 7

1. According to Noel Whelan, librarian and historian, Edenderry, the name of the man who told Ridgeway the direction which Kearns and Perry had taken was Holmes or Humes. There was a local belief that the hand with which he pointed the direction had turned into a fist, which he could not open. His family were afterwards called the 'Fisty Humes'.

2. When the rope failed to run through the loop, one of the locals present at the hanging is reputed to have shouted 'soap the rope' to those carrying out the execution. For many years afterwards, this gentleman's family was also known in the area of Edenderry by a nickname based on this advice.

Chapter 8

1. S.P. 620/39/85.
2. S.P. 620/39/86.
3. A number of the Wexford rebels managed to lie low until conditions returned to normal and many remained in the area and lived out their lives there. Some of them married local girls and their families survived. Apart from Coffey and McEvoy, mentioned by John Kiely, and Kelly, whom John Gavin tells us lived at Archerstown, there are many others reported. Michael Keenan, of Glassleck, told the Irish Folklore Commission in 1941 that the ancestors of the Adams family of Shercock had come from Wexford in 1798. He said:

> In the year 1872, on August 3rd, when the first 'Green Walk' was passing through the district, a member of the Adams family came out and saluted the processionists, and provided free refreshments for several of them who had travelled long distances. The family were Protestant but they always took a pride in the heroism of their insurgent ancestors in 1798. The maternal ancestors of the O'Callaghan family of Derrynure, Bailieboro, also came from Wexford in 1798. Their name was O'Reilly.

An account, written by Margaret Conway in 1960, states that families by the names of Roche, O'Hanlon, Doyle and Cashin, living in north Meath, were descended from Wexford rebels, who had settled in the district after 1798. She recounts the story of the four Hackett brothers, who fought in Meath, one of whom was killed at a bridge somewhere near Ardee. The other three managed, with help, to elude their pursuers and return to Wexford. One of them, however, returned some time later, to marry a girl from the area who had helped them make their escape. Others were not so lucky. In 1938, Bernard Gibney, then aged seventy-two, told the Folklore Commission:

> ... after the fight at Raffan some of the croppies escaped and made for Tankardstown Hill during the night and hid in some cornfields. The Yeomen found them and surrounded the cornfields where they hid. Anywhere the yeomen saw corn moving they would fire at the spot. In this way many of

the croppies were killed but their bodies were not found until the corn was cut. Three of these croppies were hanged on a gallows in the big wood of Tankardstown. Some yeomen camped on Mullaga Hill and spent their time in rounding up croppies in the district. This land was later tilled and cinders and ashes were found. These weretracks of the camp-fires. Some croppies were caught and hanged and were buried on Chamberstown Hill, since then locally called 'the British Hill'.

Joseph Price, from nearby Wilkenstown, also gave an account in 1938, when he was sixty-four, which told, 'In the western side of the townland of Ladyrath is a deep hollow called Log an Pobail. Here a wounded croppy was tended by the neighbours until fit to return to his native Wexford.'

4. S.P. 620/47/156.

Chapter 9

1. After the final confrontation at Ballyboughill, the two principal leaders remaining, Esmond Kyan and Garrett Byrne, both managed to avoid capture and, possibly together, but more likely separately, made their way back towards the south. Both Kyan and Byrne reached the rebel camp at Glenmalure, though Byrne was reported to have arrived wounded. According to an account of the events by Miles Byrne, 'It afforded a temporary and sure resting place to those brave men returning after their defeat and dispersion at the Boyne. Poor Esmond Kyan, who arrived about the same time, could not be prevailed upon to stop with us.' Kyan set out for Wexford where he was captured, tried and hanged. Much has been written in praise of Kyan and his death seems to have been widely mourned as that of a brave and courteous gentleman. Holt, leader of the Wicklowmen, also managed to make his way back to Glenmalure. It is known that Holt, with most of his County Wicklow rebels, returned to Glenmalure from Carberry, the day following the battle at Clonard. According to Luke Cullen, Holt, and his company, were amongst those, 'who deserted after Clonard'. This would seem a rather harsh judgement. Holt had never been in favour of the plan and, most probably, had this view reinforced by the failure to take the Tyrrell house. Holt surrendered himself, as did Garrett Byrne, to Gen. Moore in the Glen of Imaal on 26 July 1798. He was transported to Australia in 1800.

2. S.P. 620/39/186.
3. S.P. 620/29/41.
4. S.P. 620/39/196.
5. S.P. 620/21/2.
6. S.P. 620/79/7.

Chapter 10

1. S.P. 620/58/30.

Chapter 11

1. The people of County Meath were very concerned to mark and remember the burial places of the dead rebels throughout the county. In addition to using large stones and limewashing them to indicate their significance, there was a practice, in many places, to add to the memorial over the years. An account, given by Patrick Doggett in 1938 stated, 'There is a croppie's grave at Crock-an-Awr (near Kilbarry) and there used to be a heap of stones beside it. When people used to be passing each one would throw a pebble on it and, after a while, there was a heap of stones on the grave. The grave is there yet.'

2. I have been unable to attribute this entire section, relating to the location of graves and the stories behind them. I came across the original relevant manuscript, which is not signed, but from other references I believe it is, most likely, the work of Garda Murphy, who was stationed in Slane during the 1940s. The original documents are in the Archives of St Finian's College, Mullingar, Co. Westmeath.

Index